KNOWLEDGE ELICITATION
A Practical Handbook

KNOWLEDGE ELICITATION

A Practical Handbook

Maureen Firlej
and
Dave Hellens

PRENTICE HALL

NEW YORK   LONDON   TORONTO   SYDNEY   TOKYO   SINGAPORE

First published in 1991 by
Prentice Hall International (UK) Ltd
66 Wood Lane End, Hemel Hempstead
Hertfordshire HP2 4RG
A division of
Simon & Schuster International Group

Typeset in 10/12pt Palatino
by Witwell Limited, Southport

Printed and bound in Great Britain by BPCC Wheatons
Ltd, Exeter

Library of Congress Cataloging-in-Publication Data

Firlej, M. (Maureen)
    Knowledge elicitation : a practical handbook/M. Firlej.
      p. cm.
    Includes bibliographical references and index.
    ISBN 0-13-517145-8 (paper)
    1. Artificial intelligence. 2. Expert systems (Computer
  science)
    3. Knowledge, Theory of. I. Title.
    Q335.F563 1991
    006.3-dc20   90-23066
                                          CIP

British Library Cataloguing in Publication Data

Firlej, M. (Maureen)
    Knowledge elicitation : in practice.
    1. Expert systems. Design
    006.33

    ISBN 0-13-517145-8

1 2 3 4 5 95 94 93 92 91

Contents

Preface

The knowledge elicitation process described in this book is based on the original research of Joost Breuker and Bob Wielinga, of the University of Amsterdam, with whom M. Firlej collaborated during the Esprit Project 12: Techniques for Knowledge Elicitation and Analysis, during 1983–86. It was on the basis of this work that Breuker and Wielinga later went on to develop their methods and 'Knowledge Analysis and Documentation Structuring' (KADS) 1986–90. The techniques suggested here, though based on that work, were significantly modified through use in later knowledge acquisition projects. We concentrate on their elicitation interviewing techniques combined with practical issues and have as a result used little of their language and modelling structures in an attempt to simplify descriptions of the ideas and processes involved. However reference to their papers (Wielinga, B and Breuker, J, 1983–91) will provide detailed information of their model-driven acquisition tool (KADS) and their emerging methodology.

This is essentially a practical book intended to map out the field of knowledge elicitation for the practitioner. It is intended as a foundation upon which to build a working knowledge, based on work in the field and using more specialist books available to expand and deepen knowledge and understanding. We have tried to keep technical and academic discussion to a minimum, even at the risk of oversimplifying, because we wish to address ourselves primarily to non-specialists engaged in practical system building, rather than researchers.

We have tried to demonstrate that the skills required for accessing and understanding the knowledge of others involve subjective insight as well as objective techniques. It is not necessary to be an authority on philosophy, psychology or computer science; but the elicitor must develop the ability to use 'artistic licence' when adapting theories, techniques and ideas, to craft them into a new skill: knowledge elicitation.

Using knowledge acquisition workbenches, problem-solving shells and knowledge acquisition tools can provide a small fraction of assistance in instances where the domain and problems are well understood. 'A knowledge acquisition tool needs a clear notion of the function of the knowledge required of the system it is building so that it knows what information to ask for' (Marcus and McDermott, 1989). Many businesses and industrial centres do not have the advantages of producing systems in domains where the knowledge is homogeneous. The knowledge may be varied, uncertain and sometimes complex. The elicitor usually has to start from scratch on every project, often with a complex mixture of different people's experience. For those developing systems now, tools, and some of the more specialized techniques, are not always a practical option.

Given this situation we have emphasized the necessity of interpersonal skills required for successful interviewing. Interviewing skills can be learnt, but not primarily from books. What can be learnt from books, this one in particular, is an increased awareness of basic technique that can be used on all projects, whatever the domain, or its complexity. When this experience is combined with inter-personal skills, also developed through practice, it should result in the fruits of knowledge elicitation, that is, it should lay the foundations for useful, working systems at an acceptable cost of effort and money, delivered on time.

Acknowledgements

Our acknowledgements and thanks to Bob Wielinga and Joost Breuker, Annie Brooking, the reviewers and colleagues who gave helpful advice in the drafts of the book, all those who assisted in its preparation, and those from whom we gained our knowledge.

1 Some initial factors in knowledge elicitation

1.1 INTRODUCTION

1.1.1 Problem definition

It is now almost a cliché in the literature of knowledge based systems that knowledge elicitation is a problem (Hayes-Roth et al., 1983; Evans, J. St., 1988). Since it is the intention of this book to contribute towards a solution, or at least, ameliorate part of the problem, it would be worthwhile to spend some time examining and defining the nature of this problem.

1.1.2 The expert

Expertise is usually predicated of a person. There may be many possible sources of knowledge: books, recordings and so on, but expertise usually implies an expert. And experts, being experiencing subjects just like the rest of us, bring something of their individuality to the knowledge they possess.

All the incoming raw material of the expert's perceptions are filtered through the sum of the effect of all previous individual experience, combined with aspects of their cognitive equipment and make-up which were given at birth. Hence for better or for worse knowledge is marked with individuality, and, while it is possible to hold both knowledge and experience in common with other people, the expert's is uniquely linked to personality as a whole.

1.1.3 Learning expertise

It would be instructive to look, informally, at the processes involved in learning expertise. A simple example within many people's experience should suffice, that of the expertise required in writing a technical paper or report. Where universal literacy is the norm, most people will be able to write. Technical writing is a more specialized subset of this skill, with its own set of guide-lines and parameters which the author observes and absorbs in the course of reading and writing papers.

During the course of that development, probably from school, the average practitioner has to learn a great deal, from the basic manipulation of language, to the more specialized skills such as constructing a grammatically correct sequence of paragraphs to convey clearly the meaning the writer wishes to impart. This process starts consciously, as do most learning processes, and with experience and practice becomes more automatic. Thus it is quite difficult for many people to remember what it felt like to take the first steps when learning to write.

It follows that the further we proceed with a learning process, the less conscious it often becomes. Beginning students may labour long and hard over report writing, and only with time gain more fluency and confidence. Experienced professionals are able to do such a task almost without thinking about the form, channelling most of their effort to conveying the substance, simple judgements about structure having become almost automatic.

From this example we can draw out some useful generalizations about expertise. Learning many forms of expertise starts with a conscious effort and, with experience, becomes increasingly automatic. Raw data and experience is combined mentally into block processes (in psychological language, 'schemas') which can be called upon almost without conscious thought when a familiar task is performed.

These schemas can be modified and refined by further experience. The process of learning and becoming expert involves building knowledge into schemas, a kind of framework or mental outlook (Rumelhart, G., 1980).

So an expert is likely to have well established patterns of thinking that have become submerged by habit. There is no reason for the expert to carry a conscious model of how he or she thinks, experts are valued simply for being efficient at performing their skill, not understanding how or why they do what they do. Yet that is precisely what the elicitor needs to know if a successful emulation of the expert's behaviour is to be constructed.

1.1.4 The elicitor

The elicitor has the task of making the content and processes of the expert's knowledge manifest again, uncluster the components which hang together to make the expert's knowledge work. The elicitor must rediscover the paths and process of the expert's learning, specifically where it is used to complete a particular task(s).

The elicitor is not only required to grapple with more theoretical aspects of human thought, its processes and structures, but also with the realities of real world people, who possess knowledge and experience, have personalities, feelings, views and so on. This may seem obvious, yet if it is, this has not been reflected in the rush to formalize, mechanize and quantify every aspect of knowledge elicitation. Formal aspects must be incorporated in structuring the results of elicitation interviewing, analysis and the pre-machine implementation stage, but they should not encroach on the elicitor's relationship with the expert. Knowledge elicitation is, we believe, essentially a qualitative process with analytical and quantitative aspects. This is why we stress the interview as the central, practical tool for successful elicitation.

1.1.5 A communication model

We observed above that incoming information is filtered through the residual grid of previous experience, in the form of various types of schemas which make up the individual's cognitive apparatus (see Fig 1.1). This model provides a more or less coherent framework of mental sets, expectations and orientations for receiving and effectively processing new information. It also allows for the existence of negative interactions, where communication fails in one or other of the parties, or both. This can lead to bias, misunderstandings, false assumptions and the like. In any interaction between the expert and elicitor the chances of misunderstanding, or of failing to communicate efficiently are potentially great, and grow with any degree of size and complexity. This is a significant problem for knowledge based systems precisely because they are often dependent on human beings being able to communicate and cooperate for their inception, encoding, and eventual performance.

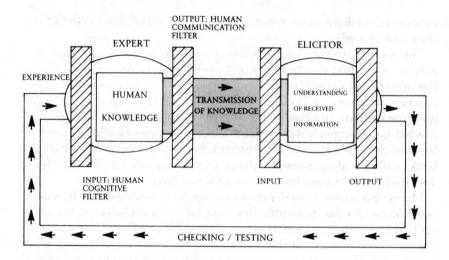

Figure 1.1   Knowledge Transmission Process

It may also be worth noting that the bottle-neck in the capture of expertise from the expertise may be as much due to overambition as much as any inherent problem in understanding how experts encode their knowledge. What we can do, practically, in addition to trying to understand the expert's thinking, is ensure that there are realistic and practical limits on the systems we are trying to build. Using these limits it is possible to build systems that perform useful tasks within a practicable framework.

1.1.6 The nature of knowledge

The successful practice of knowledge elicitation does not, para-doxically, rely on understanding the nature of knowledge. Such understanding has eluded philosophers for as long as epistemology has been an active branch of philosophy. As far as practising knowledge elicitation skills is concerned it is a very much smaller subset of human knowledge that is relevant.

We must understand what human experts know so that we can emulate some aspect of their performance on a machine. The machine does not need an entire world view, life experience, or even all the expert's specific knowledge (about an area of expertise). It performs a given task, within constraints, for a given purpose. Nor does the machine need to carry out the task in exactly the same way experts do as long as it simulates a degree of accuracy agreed by those concerned.

The nature of knowledge itself in a philosophical sense, though it may be of interest to others, is not dealt with here. We maintain that the nature of expert knowledge is adequately defined, for our practical purposes, by the practice of attempting to understand it for machine emulation. To paraphrase A. J. Ayer: 'Knowledge elicitation is what knowledge elicitation does'. This is sufficient definition here because the application of the procedures and skills advocated in this book will elucidate enough about expert knowledge in a given domain for the successful practice of knowledge elicitation.

Much the same considerations apply to knowledge of human psychology. As far as successfully practising knowledge elicitation skills is concerned, understanding the way the mind works is useful, but knowledge of all the theories that have ever been proposed will not necessarily guarantee adequate results from knowledge elicitation, either in obtaining the right information or the right amount of it. The practitioner needs to know where and how to apply this knowledge. This can best be learned by getting involved in a project and gaining real experience.

Short of having the whole process of knowledge acquisition automated, a prospect which is not easy to foresee in the near future, communication between human beings remains important, and, we maintain, a vital element of knowledge elicitation.

It is assumed throughout the book that verbal communication is still the main method of obtaining or imparting information. However unquantifiable, unscientific and apparently unsatisfactory it may seem, it provides the most basic, the most flexible, the most subtle means of communicating information, experience and ultimately knowledge. And, as has always been the case, it can be done well or badly. This book attempts to provide some understanding of the elicitation process and a framework within which to do it well.

1.1.7 Methodology

Commercial and business requirements create different demands than research development projects and the laboratory. The synthesis report (Esprit 12) claims that 'it should be possible to use people who are not necessarily skilled in all areas of KBS'. They maintain, as we do in this book, that workers skilled in a sub-set of knowledge should work as a team, thus allowing system developments to benefit from shared congruence, experiences and diverse expertise. The development task can thus be implemented by partitioning or modularization.

This partitioning can prevent, or soften, the problems due to workers leaving projects during its life span, and other participators can be replaced with the minimum of disturbance to the team. With many of the knowledge based systems embedded into other conventional systems (Mainframes, networks, data managing and semi-diagnostic systems, and those residing with production or in-house systems), partitioning of tasks is now becoming almost essential.

One of the fundamental issues is that our methods challenge the common assumption that practitioners must understand knowledge representation formalisms as an essential prerequisite to knowledge elicitation. For small scale projects it may well be practical to know something of knowledge representation formalisms, but such knowledge might equally prove a restriction on the elicitor's thinking, preventing the elicitor from seeing the domain knowledge without preconceptions, these being imposed, consciously or subconsciously, by bias towards representation issues.

Knowledge acquisition — knowledge elicitation — knowledge engineering

The above terms are all used interchangeably throughout expert system literature. The terms acquisition and engineering more usually include the design and implementation stages of building an expert system, e.g. 'knowledge acquisition is an investigative experimental process involving interviews, protocol analysis, and re-formulation of written materials in order to design computational, quantitive models of systems' (Gaines and Boose, 1987). Also, 'Knowledge acquisition is the process of acquiring knowledge and building expert systems' (Feigenbaum and McCorduck, 1984). Nancy Cooke and James McDonald in their paper of 1986, say 'knowledge acquisition is quite general, often ambiguous, and includes knowledge elicitation techniques, as well as machine learning approaches . . . an alternative solution is to improve upon the techniques available for extracting knowledge from human experts'.

In this book we refer to knowledge elicitation as a subset of knowledge acquisition. Elicitation is specifically the process of drawing forth, or evoking a reply from the human expert for the purpose of building a system.

Expert system — knowledge based system

While some practitioners wish to maintain a distinction between these terms, others are content to use them interchangeably. We believe that any such distinction applies to issues of system application only. Since this book is primarily concerned with acquiring information prior to its formulation on a machine we make no such distinction between the two terms and use them interchangeably throughout the book.

2 The elicitation process

2.1 STRUCTURING THE ELICITATION PROCESS IN PRACTICE

2.1.1 Why structure the elicitation process?

The elicitor will be under much pressure to establish the nature of an expert's knowledge as quickly as possible. Because of this it may be a temptation to muddle through, rather than planning a coherent structure to the process.

2.1.2 Pressures for success

There are two kinds of pressure that the elicitor should be wary of:

• using ad-hoc methods (Veryard, R., 1986)
• failing to plan the project properly.

Let us consider each of these pressures in more detail.

2.1.3 Ad-hoc methods

The elicitor is sometimes put under pressure to get results which can be implemented as quickly as possible (Broadbent, D., 1971). This pressure is often difficult to resist in practice. It occurs as soon as any progress is made in knowledge acquisition and something has been firmly established about the expert's skill. It is always very tempting to begin hacking the system implementation immediately, leading to piecemeal development, largely unplanned, or only vaguely with no specified end point other than a successful implementation (Elio, R., and Anderson, J. R., 1981). Note though, we are not referring to proper, incremental prototyping, which is a sound means of system building in an appropriate context.

But practitioners should be aware that changes are possible in knowledge as it is revealed and better understood. There is an inherent danger of wrongly extrapolating from the current state of understanding to the final correct interpretation (Smith, E., et al. 1978). This is a common occurrence where there is any degree of sophistication in the knowledge. Ad-hoc methods require continued revisions, updates, or worse, a complete redevelopment of the system, a time consuming and potentially costly process. Later stages of refining the knowledge representation can affect profound changes in the way the knowledge, and its subcomponents, fit together and give rise to effects which ripple back and reshape an earlier understanding of the expert's task, methods or domain.

Until an agreed representation of the expert's performance is acquired (or as much as is required for a planned stage of development of the system) the course of elicitation is contingent on a final, agreed and hopefully tested interpretation, or at least an accurate overview of it. The stages of elicitation are always provisional then, and may be subject to subtle, though often profound and far-reaching change in the light of subsequent work (Clancy, W., 1983). In our experience this can be the case even in the most (apparently) simple or straightforward looking cases.

2.1.4 Pitfalls in planning

The second pressure which should trigger alarm bells in the mind of a practitioner is that of being constrained by visible productivity. In conventional data processing circles planning has become, probably reasonably, totemistic: almost every step of the development of a conventional computer system should be accompanied with something that can be planned for and delivered to provide evidence of progress. This can be a useful and successful means of staying in control, and tracking progress. But attempts to apply this sort of strict productivity control to the less well defined and developed area of knowledge elicitation, an area beset with often hidden difficulties and unknown problem depths or limits, is misguided. To transfer too rigorous standards and expectations could cause serious and unforeseen problems, however desirable and well intentioned the aim of such planning originally was. Planning methods need to be adapted to the special requirements of the elicitation task, a procedure which requires some thought and consideration.

However well defined the ultimate goal, it cannot be guaranteed that the steps towards it will be predictable, uniform, homogeneous or even necessarily easily identifiable. The process of elicitation is seen as a problem, or 'Bottle-neck' (Hayes-Roth, B. Waterman, D. and Lenat, D., 1983) precisely because the knowledge is not well defined, and unpredictable factors make planning and time estimation more difficult. Such practical problems as: the lack of uniformity in domain types, inarticulate or unco-operative experts, or the widely varying degrees of knowledge depth among experts, within and between fields of expertise, (an expert may cover a large field of knowledge in a shallow fashion or a very narrow area in great depth, hence the description of 'wide and shallow' and 'deep' knowledge), and so on. For these reasons, traditional formulae for planning and time estimation are less likely to be accurate even with wide experience, unless the variables are very similar.

2.1.5 Control, validation, accuracy and completeness

For any given expert domain, there are always the general problems of control, validation and accuracy of the information elicited.

Controlling the quantity of information can often be as crucial as its accuracy. Even where information is accurate, it is all too easy to be swamped by information volume and lose sight of the overall pattern (Adelson, B., 1984). Even though adequately prepared, apparently, the elicitor can easily fall into the trap of abstracting vast amounts of information at each interview, but then get lost in an abundance of unclassified or unsifted information which is un- covered. It is not only a question of the right information, but of the right amount at the right time, then control of the whole process is maintained.

The feeling of being overwhelmed by incoming information, even though things are apparently going well, makes elicitation subjectively harder than it really is, and involves the elicitor in more effort, stress and worry than is truly necessary.

The prospective elicitor will have to consider the following issues, the significance of these questions will become more apparent throughout the book.

- What type of information is required, from which area, what depth and/or breadth is required? Does the expert understand the limits that the elicitor has set? How difficult is it to work within these limits?
- Whether the information gathered is relevant for the particular stage of elicitation.
- How significant the information is, both in relation to what has been gathered so far and in relation to understanding the whole.
- Whether the information seems complete, and if so what steps have been taken to validate it? Does the environment contribute to task validation for instance?
- Is the information relatively complete, as far as potential system function requires it to be? Will the system have the knowledge to perform its task without fault, failure, ambiguity or inconsistency?

It is not that the expert will deliberately attempt to deceive the elicitor, merely that our expert may not understand how to supply the right information, or how much to supply and by what method. Experts may, in good faith, believe that they have provided what an elicitor seeks, whereas in fact the information is only partially accurate over major cases, say, or is good textbook theory but not reflected in the expert's actual practice.

The pedigree of all information given must always be checked. But it is also necessary to be subtle. Experts have often spent a great deal of time and effort in acquiring their expertise, and are therefore justifiably proud of their knowledge. It is not good elicitation practice persistently to cross examine an expert as if what was said about their performance is obviously misleading (even if it is!), other methods should be used for verification purposes.

2.1.6 Information explosion

We have noted the problem previously, that experts do not always 'know what they know'. The task of eliciting knowledge is seldom a linear passage from start to finish, but rather a maze in which it is easily possible to go down blind alleys, misunderstand ideas, get distorted information, and spend valuable time collecting irrelevant data. A great deal of work may be done, much of which is of no particular use, and information collected, some of which may be irrelevant or wrong.

Further the elicitor may need to consult sources other than just the expert. Information may be required from those who consult or interact with the expert ('users' or other experts). Books, manuals or other written sources may have to be consulted, or additional observations of some aspect of the domain may have to be made. This makes the proliferation of information even more of a problem.

What follows is a discussion of how to structure the process of elicitation, in order to help avoid these problems, and ensure the elicitor can stay in control of projects (Belnap, N., 1976).

2.2 DOMAIN VIEWS

The basic ideas put forward here for decomposing a domain are based on the work of Breuker and Wielinga (Breuker and Wielinga, 1983–91) and the development of their 'objects of analysis'. A Domain View, as we have developed the idea, is like a perspective or angle of vision, to allow us temporarily to sub-divide the expert's knowledge. This is of course not necessarily a reflection of any underlying mental reality within the expert's knowledge, nor necessarily within a recognized structure within the domain.

We suggest some basic Domain Views to illustrate our approach, though these are not intended to be the only possibilities, as should emerge from the discussion below. These basic Domain Views are:

1. The Expert.
2. The Knowledge.
3. The Environment.
4. The Users.
5. Project Requirements.

The elicitor may wish to add to, or supplant, those suggested above by identifying more natural divisions within the domain if a more natural perspective readily suggests itself. Otherwise, we recommend the above categories.

The elicitor can then concentrate on each of the sectors, focusing the collection of information and, at the same time, restricting the flow into manageable proportions.

Depending on the size of the project, these sectors can in turn be decomposed. The elicitor can thus consciously vary the degree of generality by dividing the information obtained under categories. For example, dividing category 2 (domain knowledge) into, say, static knowledge: the 'what' aspect of the knowledge (facts concepts and so on); and strategic knowledge (the 'how' aspects; procedures, strategies and the like).

The elicitor may consider any kind of division that proves helpful in a working context, so long as it is recognized that these divisions are mostly a convenience and do not always reflect the holistic nature of the expert's understanding.

2.2.1 Overview

Using this series of views applied in turn to shape and focus the questioning, elicitors can concentrate on exploring more manageable amounts of knowledge, at the level of detail they have chosen. As an elicitor's understanding develops, they can increasingly integrate their understanding until finally able to understand the whole, under guidance from the expert.

Viewing the domain in this segmented way provides an effective means of control, freeing the elicitor from the need to comprehend too much too soon, and allows effort to be concentrated on developing the subtlety and penetration of the questioning strategy, or on assessing feedback from the expert's answers (the issues of an effective strategy for questioning will be dealt with later in the chapter).

During the opening stages of elicitation, the initial questions asked are general, chosen to reveal high level information about a particular area or aspect of the domain. These general views of the domain provide the scaffolding upon which successive layers of detail can be added, blocking in the elicitor's 'picture' of the domain. The elicitor asks increasingly sophisticated and detailed questions and towards the end, the fine details can be more confidently filled in, the relationships, dependencies and cross-references sorted out, until the picture is complete.

The larger the domain in question, the more important these considerations become. Where there are several experts who must be interviewed or the knowledge is very heterogeneous in nature, thinking and planning carefully how the segmentation is done becomes more essential. But even in simpler domains, segmentation can still increase efficiency.

2.2.2 Determining the sections of the domain

We will make some recommendations below of a general scheme for segmenting a domain. This is largely to illustrate the technique and provide some ideas of how useful sections might be identified. It should be stressed, however, that the process of partitioning should be driven by the context of a particular domain. The sections suggested are not supposed to be normative or prescriptive, nor can the process of division be done automatically or without thought. The suggestions we make can also provide a useful framework on which beginners can build. They might also use the suggested divisions to test for adequacy of coverage and degree of fit, or to check that all the important areas are covered. But always the elicitor, beginner or more experienced, must think about the domain segmentation in terms of the context, and should be prepared to think creatively as well as analytically.

The emphasis must always be to maintain the integrity of the knowledge, and avoid distorting the domain. A balance between the dictates of control and efficiency on the one hand, and the integrity of the information obtained on the other, must be kept in mind at all times. This is so because, while we are assisted by the natural propensity of the mind to find structures and uncover patterns in all things, it is not always the case that these discoveries are accurate reflections of any original patterns in the mind of the expert (Miller, G., 1956). The elicitor may create a new pattern by misconception. Distortions can easily creep in. As pattern finding seems to be the basis of our perception of the world, the elicitor should always be mindful of the possibility of mismatching perceptions.

2.2.3 Five sectors for viewing a domain

The order of the sectors, although not absolute, is not accidental (see Section 2.2.2). There is a useful natural progression from the expert to the knowledge possessed, treated here as if it were something in its own right (which in terms of a model representation it will become); then to the environment of which the expertise is a part, and the users, the people directly affected by the expert, and lastly, a more general category to cover second order, but nevertheless essential, aspects of the project.

The opening stages of the elicitation process, especially the feasibility study, provide a good opportunity to begin considering how the domain is constituted. Using these divisions as a starting point during the feasibility study, it is possible to update or add section categories according to the findings from the orientation or feasibility interviews. Perhaps some sections require special emphasis, for instance, or perhaps one does not really apply. Gradually, as the elicitor gains experience, dividing and sorting process becomes more automatic, and a refinement of favoured divisions are found most useful in the working environment(s). With increasing practice it will be a technique that can be applied automatically and flexibly, in other words expertly.

But the advantage of this method is that it can be used by beginners, providing a framework while they gain experience, and allowing natural development in the course of use, and is flexible enough to be adaptable in any area. To begin with, it is used fairly consciously, until its use becomes habit.

In practice this is an enormous simplification. A given view might contain elements from other sectors, which in turn contain elements of others, etc.

2.2.4 Some examples

The following list includes examples of Domain Views with illustrative quotes taken from actual transcripts. It illustrates the kind of replies given by experts in practice. The list is not exhaustive. The examples may contain other extraneous material, such as opinions, or whether the management will support the expert system development after the prototyping stage of development, or the expert is contemplating leaving the organization. Overlaps between views occur often, these can be noted down in either of the views, what is important is that their relevance to the elicitation process and the system development has been noted and documented. A reference can be made across views if the elicitor feels this to be necessary.

The following quotes are from actual interview transcripts.

- View: objectives of the expert
  'We must know our customer's requirements, so there is a statutory obligation to get it right as well as a moral one.'
- View: knowledge about the users
  'I expect after three months, that no-one will use the expert system. I will be honest about that. But, with the turnover of staff, the expert system will be in use all the time.'
- View: knowledge about the environment
  'It sounds chaotic but it happens like that all the time; last minute improvisations, fine tuning of small detail is done at the last moment under pressure of time.'
- View: methods and theories used
  'The overall method employed is generally one of many that could be successfully used whereas the statistical analysis is based on explicit theory.'

- View: sources of information
  'All this kind of information is on that shelf, in my head, reports in Dave's office, digging through my files and published data and making a few phone calls to people I know who were there last time.'
- View: sensory modality in the expert's practice
  'One of the main things the service engineer would do in order to test the state of the machine is to look at it, look at different bits of it, what appears to be anomalous – his eyes are the main things he uses.'
- View: problems or constraints on the task
  'It is highly probable that in a few cases we don't get the full information. Experience requires noting information that is missing.'
- View: underlined strategic behaviour
  Note that this may not be detailed especially at first, but the elicitor should look for verbal clues, for instance:
  'If they send in a questionnaire, one or two things can happen.'

Make notes on any interesting information which does not seem to fall into any of the basic categories you have chosen to use. This information can often be usefully dealt with in a general requirements section, or may indicate the need for more thought and refinement of the Domain Views the elicitor has chosen to use.

2.2.5 Objections

Two common responses to these ideas from those engaged in elicitation are: 'I do this anyway' or 'It's too simple for my project'. The first objection is the most common because it is universally acknowledged as a good idea, but all too frequently not practised. As often as not the reasons are perfectly good, but the effect can be just as catastrophic regardless of whether the elicitor is guilty or in good faith. Ad-hoc organization is no substitute for proper planning, and it frequently lacks some essential elements which ensure the elicitor stays in control: for instance that they are able not only to know where they are in the process, but also what possible changes will be necessary to stay on course.

The above criticism is merely a rationalization of existing behaviour, and we note that from the transcripts we possess, particularly of beginners, but even of more experienced practitioners, the evidence contradicts this idea that segmentation is so obvious it is done anyway. True, most people do tend to concentrate on sub-problems, but often not in a manner well thought out and, frequently, not consistently applied (Dretske, F., 1983). The possibilities for chaotic results are too numerous to state individually. To give a couple of examples: confusion over conceptual categories between participants, and random changes in notation. Both of these may result in changes being made midway through one strategy without the changes being properly recorded, which in turn allows misunderstanding and confusion over plans and intentions to creep in between the participants, a factor which can easily undo the relationship between the expert and elicitor (Frenkel-Brunswick, E., 1949).

A small, systematic and conscious effort to apply a strategy, or even, if the elicitor is sure of the value of what has to be done, the effort to note down and become self conscious of the process, will repay in security and in all probability in efficiency and savings in time at the later stages of system building.

In the second case, the criticism that this strategy is too simple, is a misunderstanding of the subtlety involved in such apparently simple ideas. While it is true that the basic idea is simple, at least simple when described on paper, it would be unwise to assume that it is a simple matter to apply in practice. But no technique worthy of the name ever is. This is where the skill of elicitation lies. If we advocated merely applying the same categories inflexibly to all cases, this might indeed be a valid criticism, but, as the preceding and following discussion should make clear, the divisions suggested above constitute only a notional starting point, to be applied thoughtfully where useful, extended, modified or replaced. Psychologically it makes sense to have a definite starting point, especially when confronting the unknown, as the elicitor usually is, even if this start is abandoned or quickly changed. The mere fact that it has been abandoned or changed implies that our understanding has developed.

Focusing in turn upon each of these general headings, we can generate the kind of information that is likely to be required, or come to understand why that category is less useful and replace it with one that arises more organically from the emerging knowledge and model of the expert's behaviour.

We will discuss domain segmentation next, and show how it can be used as an effective means of: keeping the elicitor in control of an interview, and aware at all stages where they have got to, and where they are going; enabling the elicitor to work out, if up-dates and/or changes are required, what effect they might have on the future course of the elicitation process. Let us now consider in more detail the views suggested in Section 2.2.2, to give a clearer idea of what sort of information they would be expected to yield and how it helps the elicitor structure the work.

2.3 VIEWING THE DOMAIN IN PRACTICE

2.3.1 View 1: The expert

What is an expert, and how are they identified? What are their skills and how can they be recognized? Unfortunately there are no clear definitions. An expert is usually 'recognized' as one, effectively by acclaim, based on experience. Their skills are usually apparent in a particular context and distinguish them from others who do not have their level of experience (Murphy, G., 1984).

The clearest way of defining an expert is to describe the qualities they use in their problem solving behaviour. Experts have:

• extreme flexibility
• organizational skills
• a wealth of knowledge of their domain
• the ability to make effective use of this knowledge
• different strategies to hand for different types of problems
• a tendency to formulate their knowledge in a declarative way
• ad-hoc methods

Experts rarely talk in vocabulary that is readily formulated into rules, and may have difficulty in explicating their problem-solving strategy (Wielinga and Breuker, 1983–91).

Experts may have special skills in public speaking, or mathematical skills, diagnostic or organizational skills, motor skills, etc., or a combination of them, some, but not all of these skills can be emulated in an expert system.

Approaching the expert

Initially, as well as gathering information, we need to establish a good relationship with our expert(s) and make them feel comfortable with the process of elicitation. It is useful to start with some easy, general questions about the expert and their role within the domain. Most people feel comfortable talking generally about what they do. Starting in this way has the advantages that:

- The expert is allowed some time to settle and get used to the idea of the elicitation process itself.
- The elicitor can assess the general high level of information, at this orientation stage, for useful signposts and warning signals about the domain knowledge which can be fed back into future sessions.
- The elicitor can also take the opportunity to examine the expert's responses to questions for clues about their character, disposition, preferences and ability to verbalize in order to assist the expert to be more comfortable with the whole idea of elicitation.

Suggesting this inevitably sounds manipulative, yet it is in everyone's interest that the process goes smoothly, and some forethought and effort be made initially to anticipate the expert's needs and potential problems. Further it is wise to ensure that the elicitor is aware of anything that is likely to affect the process adversely.

The expert's function

The elicitor's opening questions, and the transcripts that result from them, are not just warm-up exercises that can subsequently be ignored. They will provide crucial information on the expert's function. Where an expert system is the final goal, properly emulating the function of the expert is at the heart of the system development process (Shaw, M.).

It might be, for instance, that the expert fills a much wider role than is required by a simple expert system application. Yet the elicitor must know how to ensure that the system properly emulates the expert's behaviour and responses. Otherwise users may be confused by the system, and be slow to take it up, or even refuse to use it, preferring the better understood responses of the human expert, even though his knowledge has been successfully captured in the expert system.

The expert's task

The elicitor also wishes to know what the nature of the expert's task is, together with how the overall task decomposes into sub-tasks and problem-solving strategies (if this can be done).

The elicitor should bear in mind that it is still an overview that is required. It is often difficult to resist the temptation to dive into the details as soon as something clear about the task and its sub-components has emerged. This is precisely the time when the project will start to get out of hand: the desire to get down to detail leading the elicitor into a mass of information which cannot yet be put into a proper context.

Task classification

Hayes-Roth, B., et al, (1983) in their pioneering work on Expert Systems, identified six useful distinctions among possible tasks that expert systems perform. These are:

1. Interpretation
2. Diagnosis
3. Monitoring
4. Prediction
5. Planning
6. Design

It is possible that the expert's role does not fit neatly into any one of these categories, or that his task can only be adequately captured by a combination of them. Planning and prediction are often found together, for instance, requiring both information about the ordering of events for planning, and the frequency with which events occur for interpretation. The interdependencies between the two, especially the knowledge required to carry out either phase successfully, should be made clear at a high level from the start.

Similarly, when examining the sub-tasks, certain things should be made clear from the outset. Each sub-task may involve: a combination of different skills, knowledge about several different and heterogeneous subjects, being performed in different environments, different decisions, strategies or procedures.

The feasibility study (see Appendix A) should have defined these differences in order to establish boundaries, so that each sub-task is contained within specific problem sets. The task can, ultimately, be seen as sub-dividing into a hierarchical structure of goals and sub-goals which culminate in the final completion of the task (Hayward, S., et al., 1987).

The flow of reasoning, or the strategy that the expert uses to complete a task is analysed later in the elicitation process. It is important to know what the task is, what type of knowledge is used, where the task takes place (the environment) and something about the constraints that the performance of the task is subject to.

A brief digression on questions and their interpretation

Some questions for the elicitor to consider are given below. These questions here and in the remainder of this book, will require interpretation by the elicitor on the context of the specifics of a given project. An elicitor cannot simply ask the question and expect straightforward answers that will solve all outstanding problems. The elicitor must be prepared to interpret that result.

The questions are intended to draw attention to possible areas for further elicitation, and to problems that might arise in those areas. The questions are simply indicators of where best the elicitor should direct attention. Obviously the specifics of a given project will indicate how much thought about possible contextual modifications is required before the questioning strategy is tuned for the best effect.

Readers should therefore treat the questions as signposts to direct their thinking about given problems, to explore for potential problems or problem areas where more information will be required, given that only they know how the answers will impinge on their domain 'views', (project requirements, user, expert, environment and knowledge).

Questions to ask about the task are:

1. Is there one main task or several smaller related tasks?
2. Are the sub-tasks performed in different environments?
3. Are there any variations in the knowledge for each of the sub-tasks?

There may be constraints on the expert performing the task. Such constraints should be made explicit as soon as possible, so that adequate consideration is given to the means by which a putative expert system can compensate for them, using backtracking, or installing reasonable default strategies for instance. Certainly the system must cover reasonable constraints on a solution, to notify the user when its solution is less reliable than the expert's.

The expert's thinking

Obviously thinking is a highly individual process. It is often the case that people have preferred strategies of thinking (Kolodner, J., 1983). This may be a result of background and training, such as a preference for working with figures and quantification which is often a necessary part of the domain. Further there are equally significant preferences, such as whether the expert thinks visually, or verbally, or mostly abstractly, or analogically, and so on (Henderson, J. and Nutt, P., 1980). How comfortable will the expert feel with diagrams or analogies? Does a preferred style of thinking arise directly as a result of the domain or is it a matter of personal style? Such questions can often be usefully addressed at the early stages, and successfully identifying preferences can greatly enhance both good preparation and efficient information transfer.

There are many different ways of approaching and solving problems and it would be an extensive study in itself to attempt to capture and analyse even a few of them. The scope of this section is far more modest: we attempt to capture some useful generalizations abstracted from watching experts in practice to see what information we can glean (Wilkins, D., 1904).

1. Classification ('What am I dealing with?')
It is common for the expert to do some prior general analysis. The expert might assess, for instance, whether the problem has been met before. The first stage proper begins with the expert undertaking a general perusal and attempting to classify the problem. The expert looks for the elements that are familiar and unfamiliar since both will provide clues to the solution.

2. General Initial Hypothesis ('It could be this')
Assuming that enough information has been generated, the expert is in a position to choose an initial hypothesis. It is likely that there are several possibilities in mind but one in particular recommends itself as more promising than any of the others.

3. Further Analysis ('This is important, this isn't — what do I need to know?')
The expert can begin to assess the problem in the light of a hypothesis. The expert can eliminate aspects which are not relevant if the hypothesis is correct, and isolate those aspects which definitely are important. The expert also looks for information not present which is needed if the problem is successfully solved.

4. Testing the Hypothesis ('I look to confirm or confound the idea')
The expert can now subject a hypothesis to test. The expert devises tests to confirm or refute the hypothesis. The tests may not be exhaustive or conclusive, but the expert's experience should tell whether or not it is on the right lines, or whether a modification or a change to the hypothesis would be better.

If it looks as though the initial hypothesis should be rejected, the expert may backtrack to any of the previous stages, perhaps looking at the original analysis again, and choosing a new candidate hypothesis for testing. The expert repeats this cycle as often as necessary, although it is unlikely to happen many times unless the problem is outside normal experience, or there is insufficient information to work with.

5. Confirmation ('I like this idea')

Eventually one of the candidate hypotheses will emerge as leader (even if it is that the problem cannot be solved). The expert now tests the leading hypothesis extensively to confirm it. At the same time beginning to examine the implications of it being true, and any consequences of this.

The expert's thinking in action

It is misleading to think of the expert as being perfectly clear-headed about all aspects of the domain. It is not uncommon for experts to work extensively in a particular part and become rusty in less well used areas. For example, an expert on computer hardware might deal only with certain makes of machine. When such experts come back to areas they have not worked in for some time, updating their knowledge will be needed, especially since the machine architecture may have developed and changed since the last encounter.

Similarly, if certain types of problem keep recurring, it is likely that a practitioner's expertise will become stronger around those problem types. A different kind of problem could stretch the expert, necessitating revision or fresh learning. In fact, experts may go on learning about their chosen field for as long as they are in practice. An expert who can easily solve any problem in a domain might well feel unchallenged and consider moving on to some other areas, especially if expertise can be transferred in whole or in part.

Experts often think 'in motion'. This is especially important when analysing transcripts or listening to experts talk because they say things that appear inconsistent. Their description starts with an initial characterization of some aspect and in the course of describing it in more detail, their final characterization differs in important respects. Some novice elicitors get very impatient with these in-consistencies and yet it is seldom that the expert has really misled them. It might be that different levels of description are inexplicably causing a descriptive inconsistency, or that the expert has switched from one means of characterization to another. It is not uncommon for one problem to be described in several different ways which change the focus or the level of detail. The problems of managing a warehouse, for instance, would look completely different to a management consultant and an insurance underwriter.

Other factors

It may be that there are other factors at work which reflect on the expert's thinking. Does he rely on information from external sources and act, in effect, as a mediator or interpreter between a large body of knowledge and the people who require answers? Is the expert's role more one of judgement or heuristic intuition? Are heuristic judgements based on knowledge called upon? and, if so, were they devised or inherited? More generally, how much awareness does the expert possess of what, how and why things are done? We already know that experts may not 'know what they know', but it may also be that because of informal training, or trial and error learning, they are not even aware that there is anything in principle to know about. Yet this is precisely what the elicitor must reveal and they must learn to read between the lines when trying to understand the expert's thinking.

Certainly, the degree of ease with which experts are able to articulate what they do, and how they do it, will influence the elicitor's plans when assessing the suitability of different techniques and tools. Where it is obvious that an expert has difficulty expressing knowledge, the elicitor should consider some techniques other than interviewing, such as psychometric methods, to illustrate the relationship and dependencies between major concepts. But bear in mind that flexibility is required; an articulate expert might find psychometric techniques frustrating and alienating.

Agreement among experts

When questioning an expert, we need to know how well agreed is the information that the expert provides, among his/her peers. For the purpose of expert system building, there needs to be a limit put on how much disagreement is tolerable between experts (Boose, J., 1986). For example, in a traditional western medical system, gross differences of opinion between western doctors over the cause and therefore the diagnosis and treatment of a disease would cause insurmountable problems for a system, even where used in conjunction with a doctor. Different medical paradigms would necessitate different systems depending on what medical model (herbalist, acupuncture, etc.) was the basis from which the expert worked.

Other factors may have some bearing on agreement between experts (Mittal, S. and Dym, C., 1985). For example, the role of the expert: a surgeon may have a different view of patient's needs from that of the patient's local general practitioner. Similarly their view about treatment, will reflect their different levels of expertise, and in many cases will not overlap.

The elicitor should check on the status of opinion among the expert's peers. It is usual for some disagreement to occur between experts, but the elicitor must quickly identify an acceptable limit for difference within the domain. If there are discrepancies in the system any practical use is limited.

Differences of opinion often reflect the fact that experts are taking different information into consideration in order to establish a 'truth', or they may be giving different 'weightings' to the same information. Thus the specific information and its source should be established and checked to see if there are any irreconcilable differences of expert opinion.

Consider another example. A system incorporating the expertise of an economist may be very difficult to implement. Economists may disagree as to what concepts or trends they need to take into consideration when they make a financial forecast, and they may still disagree even if they are given the same data or goal. In a teaching system, or a consultation system, this may not cause great difficulty, it may even enhance its usefulness. Whereas in some decision-making systems it might cause difficulty.

There are also limits and conditions which may curtail the user's or expert's choice; the elicitor should be aware of this in the early stages of the feasibility study. The elicitor should ask the following questions about agreements or disagreements:

1. Do experts agree on what are the concepts of the domain knowledge?
2. Do experts have 'opinions', which differ from other experts?
3. Is there only one 'right' decision or way to perform a task?

Is the expert available?

So far we have assumed that access to an expert is straightforward and automatic. Rather than several experts in disagreement, it may be that the elicitor has difficulty getting hold of an expert at all. Experts may be scarce because:

- Training is long-term (as in the case of doctors for instance).
- Experience is difficult to acquire.
- There are few practising experts even though there is a need for them, and they are busy, or out of the vicinity.
- They are highly specialized, and the domain is split up into different sub-areas of expertise which cut across the total area you wish to consider.
- Their expertise is confidential or exceptionally valuable and the expert or his managers may not wish to lose control of it.
- There may be a recruitment problem.

- The expert may not wish to participate in elicitation.
- There may be departmental divisions or corporate strategies which may prevent cooperation between expert and elicitor.

Obviously this list is not exhaustive. Such problems will require very careful thought to devise the most efficient means of getting information from the expert(s), or in devising some other means to elicit the required information.

2.3.2 View 2: The knowledge

The second important view of the domain concerns the domain knowledge, considered in the abstract as if it were an independent entity.

First and second order knowledge

In the ensuing discussion we will occasionally distinguish between first and second order knowledge. First order knowledge is that which experts possess and manipulate, and which is referred to in the bulk of the discussion just as 'knowledge'. In effect this is the expert's ability to solve problems, or carry out tasks and then explain what was done and why. Second order knowledge, or meta-knowledge, is that which the elicitor seeks, knowledge about the expert's knowledge, procedures, reasons, heuristics and so on, that is, how the expert carries out the task, 'knowing about what the expert knows'.

The first case consists of the model or models that an expert has of a domain. The second case consists of a developing model of the expertise that the elicitor is building. It is rare that experts, or anyone else, have a precise model of their own practices, the meta-knowledge, and experts who think they have such knowledge can often turn out to be wrong about their ability to explain their own special knowledge and how they use it (Adelson, B., 1984). The former, first order knowledge may be public, the latter, second order knowledge seldom is. Yet it is this second order knowledge, this normally opaque area, held outside the conscious range of most people, which is of interest to the elicitor. Revealing it can be a frustrating experience: examination of transcripts by novice and even some more experienced elicitors reveals that their frustration and impatience to 'get hold of something' can lead to serious error: misreading explanations, imposing premature and false perceptions and, worst of all, offending the expert with displays of impatience and petulance. Offending the expert is always unwise.

But there are symptoms that can give the elicitor clues to the existence of hidden knowledge. Frequently, when answering questions, the expert seems to wander aimlessly over his area of expertise and does not, on the surface, seem systematically to apply any rules or principles. He might even deny that there are any, but such statements should not always be taken at face value.

A proof reader, for example, may skim a chapter so fast it seems impossible that he could comprehend the information it contained. Yet when tested his comprehension appears to be very good. But he is unlikely to be consciously aware of the cues and triggers he uses to assimilate the essential information so quickly as he skims: topic sentences, key words, section headings and so on. He has integrated such strategies into the fluent performance of a skill, he is an 'expert' at speed reading, yet he most likely will not be able to say exactly how he performs the task, and might give a uninformative, rationalized, and even inaccurate explanation if asked (Anderson, J., 1981).

Frequently, when asked to explain what they do, experts provide only high level generalizations and seem either unwilling, or unable, to drop down to a more detailed level. Their knowledge is an iceberg where only a very small high level part is apparent at the surface of their conscious attention. There is a real danger that inexperienced practitioners can be fooled, or fool themselves, into thinking that the submerged part is less significant than it really is, or smaller than it actually is. Worse, some practitioners seem to think it doesn't exist or doesn't matter.

Static and strategic knowledge

In the case of first order knowledge, it is a common practice, and one which we will follow, to distinguish between the knowledge required for a practitioner to be considered expert, the 'what'; and the knowledge of how actually to effect the tasks, or problem solving activities in order to perform the expert's function, the 'how', that is, what knowledge the expert requires when he is performing, and how, strategically speaking, he uses it. Hereafter we shall denote these different aspects by the terms static knowledge for the 'what', and strategic knowledge for the 'how'.

This conceptual division is purely a convenience, to provide a useful handle in practical elicitation. Its usefulness far outweighs the possible danger of obscuring the reality with handy theoretical abstractions.

Using static and strategic distinctions

If we begin the process of elicitation by acquiring static knowledge only, we are likely to get more information than we actually need. If we begin with task analysis, and aim to expose the strategic knowledge, there is a real danger that we will probably understand too little of the information we get, or worse misunderstand it (see discussion on 'misunderstanding' section 3.4.2), because we have not got the requisite grasp of basic concepts and vocabulary. Problems could arise where the domain has special meanings for familiar words for instance.

So we are caught in the dilemma of understanding that the distinction does not really reflect reality, and can potentially lead to problems, especially if applied inflexibly or thoughtlessly. Yet it can also be a useful device.

We may still bring the conceptual distinction to bear during elicitation, however simply by creating heuristic guide-lines: we maintain that the static knowledge should be the subject of investigation initially, before the strategies and procedures of the expert are investigated. We attempt to encompass the static knowledge because it is so often a useful precursor to making proper sense of any strategic or protocol analysis. But this is only a matter of emphasis rather than a necessary priority. We conduct the analysis with this distinction in mind, applying it if it is useful. Because it is a guide, a conceptual tool and ultimately a convenience, it would be absurd to become enslaved by it, especially where it was proving counterproductive — though this has seldom proved to be the case so far as our experience is concerned.

Nevertheless, while the distinction between the 'what' and 'how', between static and strategic knowledge, is useful, one must always be aware during elicitation that the ultimate aim is to get an integrated view of the expert's knowledge. Sometimes it is necessary to abandon or ignore such distinctions and the expert and his expertise are treated as a whole, the whole that they are, in fact. This, inevitably, must be a judgement made in the particular context of an elicitation project.

This is only to restate one of the major themes throughout the book: there is no escape from using informed judgement when making the necessary decisions in knowledge elicitation. We believe that the process of elicitation cannot be carried out mechanically.

Human experts may have systematic knowledge of a domain, that can be discovered and mapped into a computer system, but the expert himself cannot be treated only as a 'system' to be analysed. All the subtle and complex issues of human cognition and human interaction and communication complicate knowledge elicitation and prevent it from being reduced to a problem in systems analysis.

Where such complexity is involved it is inevitable that practitioners will need to develop and use their intuition and judgement. This can be learned with practice and experience, and constitutes the art of the elicitation skill. Elicitation is itself a form of expertise, and its practice requires informed judgement, which is the essence of expertise, based on knowledge gained through experience. The use of generalizations such as static and strategic knowledge assist the elicitor in maintaining intelligent control of the elicitation process, but it must be applied thoughtfully and flexibly, dropped where redundant, and replaced by other conceptions if the context demands it.

Applying the knowledge

Although the elicitor is not consciously thinking of design and implementation matters at this stage, he may need to come to some early conclusions on whether the knowledge itself is suitable for implementation. Future implementation may demand that some important questions have already been answered (by the elicitor, from the knowledge already elicited) for the process to be continued. Severe restraints on the quality and quantity of the available knowledge, and therefore the system itself, may be brought to light by the answers these questions receive (see appendix 1. Feasibility study).

Some points to consider in the light of implementation constraints when assessing the static knowledge:

Concepts can be well defined or not very easily distinguished. They can be related to one another in a variety of ways, which can be simple or very complex. Detecting similarities and differences between concepts, and determining whether they fit into hierarchies, sets or families is a task that could be relatively simple or extremely complex.

Some points when assessing the strategic knowledge:

Most domains have several types of knowledge. With some types there may be an advantage in using conventional methods of machine implementation. Finding out early how much of the domain knowledge can be implemented in this way is an essential task for the elicitor.

Heuristic and common sense knowledge may cause user and implementation difficulties because of the lack of theoretical underpinning in heuristic knowledge and, with common sense knowledge, because of the sheer volume of mundane aspects. The extent of both types of knowledge should be assessed.

Although the elicitor usually has only one expert, it is sensible to ask if other experts agree with one another, and, if not, where the disagreements lie. A system based on totally idiosyncratic expertise, where the personality of the expert dictates the knowledge, is unlikely to be suitable for expert systems development. The extent of any idiosyncratic knowledge, if it exists, should be uncovered and assessed quickly.

Experts who disagree usually do so because they follow different methods resulting from favouring a different theory of their profession. If the experts disagree, or differ radically in the way they use their expertise, then choosing elicitation methods becomes very difficult. It maybe that the users can define the task structure within the knowledge which will solve the problem for an expert system, but if not then it may be effective to appoint an arbiter to make a decision. In practice however, experts rarely disagree about the basics of their tasks. But if they do, and options are required as a feature, then it must be incorporated into the system early.

Such questions will affect both the planning of further elicitation, and the techniques which will be required. The character of the knowledge will also affect system building considerations, especially when choosing a machine representation formalism. The answers will also assist the elicitor with clues about the way the knowledge was learned and therefore what methods can be used to uncover more of it.

Potential problems with the knowledge

Because it is important to spot problems as early as possible, these questions should be dealt with as early as possible: Do the users and the expert share a common technical language or jargon? Or does the expert have his own? This could seriously affect a later choice of screen layouts and user/system communication and also any explanation feature as clarifications of the special language will be required. How much of the knowledge is uncertain? Or variant over time? Is it possible to get independent verification for the knowledge? Is this realistic? Are there 'fashionable' theories, i.e. ones that have a tendency to change with current opinions?

If the knowledge is too unstable it will be unsuitable for systems development, but it might be useful to try to capture as much as can be found that is reliable, for teaching purposes, say. Does the expert require a great deal of real-world knowledge? Perhaps there is too much and only a small part of it can be captured. This is often the case where a real-time and efficient expert system is required. For example, it might be that an expert task consists of identifying certain grass types. The need to name one grass type, from thousands of others, all of which look extremely similar to the inexperienced eye, may require thousands of documented references in the system's memory. To know 'where' even to begin to look could be the most important component of expertise. So a vast memory and minute precision would be needed, but this may defeat the object of building a small, but useful system. Generally, it is important to consider the knowledge in the light of the purpose for which it is required. Is the knowledge complete? Is one expert enough or does the elicitor require the contribution of several experts, say, because it is a very wide and varied domain? Will the system be used by many experts for the same function, and if so, do other experts agree that the knowledge is complete, i.e., do they use the same terminology, does the task differ in some way between experts, and so on?

Experts frequently do perform the same basic task, especially within the same organization. Differences occur if the task is performed within differing contexts. In the latter case a system based on the experience of one expert is almost never enough. Bridge any gaps in the knowledge by obtaining a consensus of what the basic knowledge should be for the system. Knowledge should therefore be sought from several experts, if appropriate.

Does the knowledge require graphic representation?

The term 'graphic representation' in this context means anything which can only be adequately represented by using drawings or sketches. Some domains do have a large component of graphic content. The expert may, in the process of explaining some idea or description of a behaviour, suddenly reach for a pad and draw sketches of what he/she does, and say, 'it has to look like this!' or 'I know just by looking at the chart if something is wrong'.

Sketches and drawings may still provide a useful way of express-ing an idea on paper that is difficult to express in words, even though it may be impossible to implement the drawings physically into a knowledge based system. These sketches may be indispensable for the user and a practical method for the representation of these drawings or plans may have to be found to achieve acceptable functioning.

Does the expert rely on 'common sense' expression and explanation?

Common-sense knowledge in the usual sense implies everyday world knowledge for instance, knowledge of a 'fact'. It is sometimes true to say that what one person regards as 'common-sense' knowledge is not apparent to another. The elicitor should never assume that what the expert regards as 'common sense' knowledge is necessarily known to the users of the system.

Is the expert actually aware of why a certain thing is done? It is not always the case that experts do.[3] Some knowledge may have been received from a previous practitioner and they assume it is now common knowledge. Experts can sometimes be vague about the reasons for a decision and can sometimes resort to replies like: 'because it's always been done this way', or 'it's easier', or 'it's traditional', or, 'I was taught to do it this way and it has always worked'.

It is important to find out if the domain has much of this 'common-sense' knowledge (Kuipers, B., 1979). If it has, the elicitor must try to infer whether this knowledge has a firm theoretical or practical basis by following through some of the strategies to reach a solution. The expert may think arbitrary knowledge is used when in fact the knowledge is used judiciously (Anderson and Shrifrin., 1981).

Common-sense knowledge may be used by the expert in deciding values or probabilities. The judgements or decisions based on the knowledge may have an expected value, for example: 'yes', 'no', 'sometimes', 'depending on', etc. Can the answers be graded, for example, from 0 to 5, 200 to 2000, or low, medium, high, weak to strong, etc? If the expert finds it difficult to describe how to assess values accurately, when it is essential to be accurate, Repertory Grid techniques might prove useful (see Chapter 5 pp. 117–55).

Is the knowledge already documented?

It is essential to know whether or not the expert uses reference documents and manuals at work and, if so, how they are used, when and how much. Documents, training manuals, operating procedures, etc. may appear simple, but complex issues are hidden there, or they may create a false conceptual view of a domain. In one case, an elicitor spent days reading manuals and literature on his own initiative only to find that his reading was completely irrelevant to the part of the domain selected for system implementation. It is essential to ask the experts, at their earliest convenience, what material they suggest should be read to avoid mistakes like this.

What other types of tools or materials do the experts use during their tasks, if any? Tables and technical charts may need to be incorporated into the design of the system. Documentation of the domain indicates how far the knowledge and practices of the expert are idiosyncratic. Little or no documentation may indicate a largely unregulated way of expressing expert knowledge. Without a consistent method to act as a guide, the expert may substitute for this lack with a method of working which may be unique and different from all other experts. Documentation may provide:

• Useful back-up;
• further information on major concepts and how they relate, overlap and so on;
• an independent source of verification.

But the elicitor must take care; sometimes manuals or text books are not used in practice, or are unreliable, or not updated, and thus potentially dangerous.

Does the expert rely on any external information sources, for additional or specialist knowledge? Such information sources and their documentation (if any exists) should be discovered at the earliest stages possible, otherwise obtaining essential knowledge may incur unforeseen overheads of time and expense because of the need for extra (and possibly extensive) research, or the need to acquire special access permissions to external information sources.

Some questions concerning documentation

Are there documents that the user will have to refer to, when the system is being used? If so, are these documents already available, explicit, clear, or will they have to be adapted for use with a knowledge-based system?

How did the expert gain his expertise? Does it all come from text books, manuals or other documentation or from experience? Knowledge that is mostly gained from experience is more difficult and takes longer to elicit.

By how much, and with what knowledge, does the expert need to supplement experience from text books, manuals, etc.

Which areas of domain knowledge, or which tasks, use the most expertise and heuristic knowledge, and are therefore less likely to be well documented?

Is the knowledge theory-laden?

It is important to find out whether there is any theoretical underpinning to the expert's knowledge. If there is, is it the only theory? It is often the case that a domain requires experts to interpret ideas that are only partially understood theoretically. This may mean that experts have different ideas about 'how things should be done' in principle. The elicitor is interested in how they are done in principle and in practice, and must therefore be aware of the different possible sets of assumptions lying behind the practice of experts and what difference (if any) this will make. Often the expert will claim a theoretical position but will ignore it in practice.

This can be illustrated by considering theoretical assumptions in the domain of remedial literacy among children (Crispin, L., 1984). The 'structuralist or diagnostic' approach, which has dominated much research, relies on a set of underlying theoretical assumptions about the dependency of reading skill acquisition upon a variety of component skills. The problems of the remedial reader are specifically identified (e.g. shape recognition), and are then overcome by direct teaching initiative, or indirectly by developing alternative compensatory strategies (e.g. building up confidence, dexterity, etc).

In contrast, the task analysis approach favours the global task being broken down into successive steps, each involving a reduction in task demands. From a teaching point of view this means progressively reducing task difficulty to the point where the pupil achieves success through practising bits of the task. Success at the sub-components leads ultimately to success at the whole. The task analysis approach assumes progressive learning of each task level to the next, and task analysis skills may be appropriately applied to more specific goals within the reading curriculum.

When seen in terms of potential automated teaching aids, the first (structuralist) approach is much more knowledge based, and would, especially where indirect means were indicated, still depend heavily on the activity of a teacher. The second approach is more easy to translate into a conventional systems approach, implementing the successive small steps into a progressively applied series of reading exercises based on a hierarchical algorithmic 'yes' or 'no' structure and the appropriate action appended to a positive or negative reply. This could be achieved with conventional algorithms.

Differing theoretical assumptions in the expertise might suggest differing implicit control structures. The elicitor must make them explicit so that a decision can be made whether one is better suited for implementation in any system based on that knowledge. It may be that the different assumptions when made explicit in this way could be reconciled.

2.3.3 View 3: The 'users'

The term 'user' is used here to cover both the people who currently 'use', that is, consult the expert, and the people who will become the users of the expert system when it is built. Only when the distinction between the two groups is necessary will the reader be explicitly reminded of the difference. In most cases they will either be the same people or stand in the same relation to other aspects of the domain. Knowledge about the user is essential. The elicitor seeks information about: the knowledge a user has; how a user will apply that knowledge; and the way a user will use the system in practice. As far as most system users are concerned, the interface with which they interact constitutes that system. The Human-Computer Interface (HCI) should be clear: a consultation with the system should be at least as easily understood as one with the expert with whom the user would normally consult (even if only over a limited area). It follows that a major concern of the elicitor is to consult with actual or potential users to find out what their expectations and requirements are. Though they may not necessarily be concerned directly with the functionality of the system, users will be very directly affected by the way that functionality is accessed: through the HCI.

Many of the concerns involved in HCI development are part of the system design itself, and therefore necessarily beyond the scope of this manual. However there are some aspects, particularly those of the expert's view of relationships with the people who normally come for consultation, which can usefully be outlined and explored early on in the elicitation process.

- It is possible that the roles of 'user' and 'expert' belong to the same person.

More generally though, a system will manipulate expert knowledge to suit the needs of an actual or potential user. This consultation might be entirely different from the way the user would normally consult the expert, because of machine requirements and limitations, so it is not only the expert's view of the system or the interface that counts, a seemingly obvious point that is all too frequently overlooked. It is essential to consult the users and ascertain their needs. Therefore the elicitor should first identify the main users of the expert's knowledge, as soon as possible:

- How many of them are there, will a system greatly reduce their work and/or increase productivity in other more essential areas?
- How do the users affect the role of the expert, will a system make the expert's job unnecessary or reduce their consultancy role?
- Will there be new users of a system and will they require any education or training?

If an expert system is involved, is there likely to be resistance to it from the users? Have they been consulted about it, particularly about their HCI requirements and how they would wish to use it?

It is essential to acquire any relevant knowledge they may have which will affect them as potential users of the system, on every project.

- The elicitor should find out about a user's perception of the task or problem, and how users will want to use the knowledge in the system.
- What aspects of the task, or of the knowledge, will the users find difficult or straightforward?
- How do the users perceive their essential interests?
- Why would users normally consult experts?
- What do they need to know, and what benefits would they have if they consulted an expert system instead?

This information has a direct bearing on the use value of the system. A system that is not easy for the user to access will cause problems no matter how well it reflects the expert's knowledge and methods of reasoning.

The elicitor's perspective

Consulting the users gives the elicitor another essential perspective, assisting with such decisions, for example, as whether it is sufficient to acquire the knowledge of one expert, or to get a consensus of opinion from several, or merely inform the system's user of the existence of other experts' opinions, and allow them to proceed in their own way if required. These considerations could in turn have a very direct bearing on the efficiency of the system, an issue that will most likely be close to the heart of any user of it.

Of course there may be problems if the views of the expert and any users cannot be harmonized, especially if both will be consulting the system being built. If there is not a general consensus of opinion within the domain and the elicitor is aware of this uncertainty, preparing for its effects is essential. It may for instance be feasible to develop different modes or contexts for different users to use, like different views of a database. Different users will then have a perspective on the expertise which accords with their view of its purpose.

Inevitably, this will entail extra development cost. Where the expert is not involved with the system in use (including no role in knowledge maintenance), it is the user's requirements that should be paramount. If the elicitor and engineer adjust the knowledge to suit the view of the user however, they must take care that it does not change the basic semantics of the expert's knowledge. Changes of this nature still require ultimate validation by the expert.

Questioning users

The answers to the following questions provides the elicitor with information to help decide if the users and experts agree on some issue, and where they differ. Decisions can then be made concerning the design of the system, and who the system will serve.

Some example questions to ask about the users:

1. Do all users have the same knowledge or expertise?
The system would have to reflect the knowledge of the users, diverse knowledge would be difficult to accommodate.

2. Do different users generally agree on the knowledge?
It is essential that there is some agreement between users as the function of the system would be greatly undermined if some of the users disagreed with its knowledge.

3. Why do they need an expert system?
Can the elicitor justify the building of an expert system to the users, what reasons would be given?

4. Is the user task or their function the same for all users?
A multiple-tasked expert system would be difficult to implement, although a system can incorporate different functions quite easily. For example, a system can provide a faster and a more accurate service.

5. What are their difficulties, problems?
Do most of the users have the same problem? For example, a back-log of work or to supplement lower grade workers with extra knowledge? If they have different problems would the design of the system need to include this difference as well?

6. If the task is different for some experts in the same domain.
Why is it different and what are the causes and results of these differences? Can the elicitor reconcile these differences within one system or with more than one system?

7. How does the expert's personality alter, or enhance the knowledge?

A system that has been designed to please one expert, but no-one else will not be very useful as a tool.

2.3.4 View 4: The environment

The environment in which experts work can play a significant role, affecting the way that they perform.[13] Environmental cues can have a significant role in facilitating recall of crucial information during the expert's performance. The elicitor should consider the effects of the expert's environment as a major factor affecting their knowledge, and how it might affect the system's performance (Mitchell, C., 1989).

It is easy to miss the significance of the environment. If, for example, the expert is working on a North Sea oil platform, it is more likely that this hazardous environment will impinge greatly on the performance of a task. In an office, the effect will most likely be less pronounced, though frequently no less significantly. If the expert and elicitor share the same environmental background, it would be all too easy for these very familiar aspects to be overlooked.

Some questions to ask about the environment

When the elicitor requires more detail, the following questions should be considered.

- What influence will the environment have on the practice of the expert? Will this constrain a potential system?

- Will some resources, models or particular tools be required? Could the equipment be transferred to the place of elicitation? Might diagrams suffice to aid the elicitor to understand the expert's task?
- Could the expert explain what is done outside the normal environment? It would be unreasonable to expect a car engine mechanic to explain car mechanics without at least a model engine or prepared diagrams.
- Are there unstated assumptions about the expert's environment? For example, identifying rock structure may involve many special environmental considerations if it is being done in special circumstances, e.g. below ground in a mine or pot-hole.
- How easy is it to reproduce constraints which the expert works with and which he must take into account when performing? Is the environment noisy, and does this affect the performance of the task?
- Does the environment change according to circumstance or special conditions, and if it does, what effect does this have?

How the environment can affect expert system design

If the ultimate aim of elicitation is to produce an expert system, it is important to consider the environment where that system will be used, and to examine the consequences that consulting the system instead of the expert might have, especially where the environment differs from the original.

It makes a difference if the environments experts work in are diverse, such as an office, a factory or outdoors. It is important to ask if any of the system users have the same level of technical background and knowledge as those who consult the expert. A decision has to be made whether to have both sets of knowledge in the system. What compensatory measure needs to be considered if the expert and the user are not the same? Must this variance in the knowledge become part of the system or not?

The system environment may affect how easily the user operates the system, and how quickly, which in turn should be fed back into the design of the system.

Restrictions and constraints, such as adverse conditions of terrain, weather and so on, may have an effect on the knowledge itself by curtailing its extent as well as lowering its accuracy.

The known and perceived effects of the environment should be carefully observed, analysed and documented.

2.3.5 View 5: Project requirements

What is required from a particular project may be different for some of those involved, for example, people concerned with: project management, development management, strategic management, socio-technical and knowledge acquisition specialities. Further, some of these viewpoints may be directly in conflict with others.

It is impossible to discuss all the aspects of the planning of a project. In this book we concentrate on factors that will either mediate, or cause problems for, the elicitation part of the project. The project will, of course, involve many other aspects, and elicitation cannot be regarded as a discrete process, however, we have to scope the problem, so wider aspects are not dealt with here.

The following are aspects which the elicitor must resolve if they impinge on his ability to work efficiently, but whether the elicitor can influence events depend on a number of factors.

- whether the elicitor is consulted before the project requirements are agreed;
- whether the elicitor is consulted when the project requirements are discussed;
- whether the elicitor is consulted after the project requirements are agreed;
- if management/developers are conversant with the methods and techniques of knowledge elicitation and acquisition;
- the status of the elicitor within the company;
- the expertise and experience of the elicitor;
- the experience of the project manager.

Whether or not the elicitor has the power to influence projects so that elicitation can take place in a suitable environment is contentious. Intervention by the elicitor is often curbed. But assuming for the moment that this is a perfect world, there are several preparatory requirements that can ensure the project gets off to a good and productive start.

The elicitor must have the appropriate time in which to plan and analyse the elicitation, and to document the knowledge. Time must also be allowed later for further planning and to assist in any transfer of the knowledge. If the elicitor is not given enough time and resources, then some of the essential tasks above will not get sufficient attention.

It is not reasonable even to attempt to assess the time and resources required until something is known about the domain. In other words, not until some feasibility or orientation study has been done, since even apparently similar domains can differ in some crucial respects.

Nowadays projects can be planned within tight schedules if they are sympathetically and realistically estimated (except where the knowledge or the expert cannot be known for some reason, in which case some latitude must still be given). The KADS (Wielinga and Breuker, 1983–91) methodology suggests several modelling techniques which facilitate knowledge elicitation. The models direct elicitation and provide explanatory documentation. Documentation is therefore achieved simultaneously with elicitation.

2.3.6 Requirements associated with each view

Each type of domain will have a collection of associated requirements and problems which can be assessed in relation to the 'views' of the domain.

View 1. The expert

In most projects the expert is already assigned. Developers know enough about expert systems to initiate the choosing of an appropriate expert. Hopefully the expert is available for interviews at least once or twice a week, is articulate and motivated enough to agree (willingly) to provide expert knowledge.

Sometimes the expert is not all one would hope for, and given the choice it is usually best to initiate a change. However, this is often achieved only with considerable difficulty and is sometimes impossible. Whether the elicitor perseveres with the chosen expert or tries to suggest another more suitable candidate depends on the degree of the elicitor's influence, together with the availability or whereabouts of any other willing expert acceptable to the developers. The elicitor should be insistent if the expert's knowledge is genuinely inappropriate or insufficient for the expert system's requirements. It is imperative that the elicitor ensure the system's knowledge is as complete as possible.

If the expert is not motivated and is clearly not in a position to become so, then it is sometimes prudent to request another expert. Some experts are simply not willing to participate because of the manner in which they have been allocated to the project and show this by cancelling interviews and being obstructive. Inform the project leader or manager, if the choice of expert is not yours, of the consequences of an unwilling expert. A late change of expert may put the project behind in its schedule until someone new is allocated to the project and the preliminary procedures started over again.

If there are several experts involved in the project this will automatically lengthen the process. Experts will each require attention from the elicitor to accustomize them to the elicitation process and what is required of them within it, together with any other special demands placed on them by virtue of the shared process of elicitation.

View 2. The knowledge

In every project the elicitor must be prepared for the unexpected. A domain that uses a great deal of jargon or technical terminology obviously will take longer to learn and understand.

Some experts cannot express or explain themselves unless they use domain jargon. So it is very difficult to understand what they say about the domain and at the same time try to understand the jargon itself. Project time can be lengthened considerably if this is the case. The elicitor should give thought to alleviating this problem quickly, though if no convenient solution exists then the elicitor must be able to take the time to work through this difficulty. Showing the expert task diagrams and exploring relations between tasks may help here, but whatever the eventual outcome, some additional time will be necessary.

View 3. The environment

Mostly the environment is already set, that is, the environment in which the expert's tasks are performed. The elicitor therefore should ask: does the environment limit, or reduce in some way, the time taken in elicitation, or does noise or inconvenience interfere with the project's requirements? Will there be any difficulty in arranging the most conducive method of elicitation? Has the elicitor seen the environment? If the environment is unusual, will it be impossible to make realistic or accurate assessments of the difficulties of elicitation?

The elicitor will have to assess how each difficulty will add to the time and whether further resources are needed.

View 4. The elicitor

If the elicitor is experienced, then knowledge of some of the potential restraints and problems will be apparent. The elicitor will know how to overcome most of them. If the elicitor is new to the work, the project manager will have to take account of this fact at the pre-planning stage.

An elicitor who is new to elicitation, and who does not have the advantage of a knowledgeable project leader, should be wary of assessing any time limits. Managers usually expect their employees to keep to their estimates even though they may be inaccurate and unrealistic and therefore impossible to keep to. Don't guess or bluff on time estimates.

A way to avoid this is to break up the project's requirements into stages. For example, the first stage is 'orientation of the domain' (the views of the domain), scope the predicted time to achieve orientation and go no further. Do not extrapolate from this how long the **whole** project will take, as the chances are that your estimations will be way off. Then scope the next stage. The scoping can be done, per month (even weeks) and the details of what you hope to achieve within that month. The portions that have not been completed within a month can be scoped for the next month and so on.

Plan the stage, and what has been achieved within it, on file. This will serve as a guide and a learning device. Management will then know more or less what is achieved month by month and exactly the time taken on each item, right through until the implementation stage of the system and delivery. Scoping for the next project will then be more accurate, given the guide-lines from the first project. It may then be possible to scope the length of the whole project with more precision.

Some difficulties that occur are out of the elicitor's control. These could be slow turn around of transcripts, or even a complete halt in transcription, or withdrawal of facilities. These are administrative problems which should be solved as part of the normal project contingency plans. Time should not therefore be taken off the allotted elicitation and analysis time in order to make up the project's time slippage.

View 5. The task

Some tasks are extremely complicated, and branch out into many sub-tasks so that keeping track of the goal is difficult. Some tasks on the other hand are universally well known and they are relatively easier to follow. Experience of several domains will give the elicitor some basic knowledge about which domains will prove difficult and which prove easier. Estimates based on experience are more accurate than generalized blueprints of time estimation.

It may be helpful to examine a sample task, which will give the elicitor some idea of its complexity, and then be possible to make a provisional judgement about the majority of tasks, if they are similar.

Novice elicitors should be aware that, at the beginning of the project, not only is the effort put in greater because there are so many unknowns, or partial unknowns, but also because this is where the learning curve is highest, and the time when most problems are likely to occur. Problems must be actively sought out or they will escalate, if not recognized and dealt with at the beginning.

View 6. The sources of knowledge

Some sources of knowledge are difficult to acquire, such as rare specialist knowledge, or manuals no longer in print, code books or a source of knowledge from elsewhere. The elicitor should take these factors into account when budgeting and estimating.

View 7. Resources

It is impossible to assess individual companies' resources, so the elicitor should enquire whether the 'client' will have the right facilities for the elicitor's use. If, for example, a video is required of the expert at work, who would supply the video equipment? Other aspects such as transcription may be done by the 'client' or by the developers of the system. Some establishments like to keep the tapes of the interview on their premises. How does this affect time, and what extra resources will the elicitor need in that case? Such things should be agreed before the project begins if this is possible.

Further, the elicitor should consider how adequate some of these resources really are. The project's success could be threatened by the disorganization of the other party, for example, by losing some of your tapes and transcripts. Who is ultimately responsible for mistakes and the lack of planning on behalf of the client, and how will it affect the project?

View 8. The problems

Is it obvious when things are going wrong? Experience indicates that it is not always so. Practitioners can go quite some way, getting increasingly bogged down by details, side issues and matters of definition, before they realize how far from the path they have strayed. Worse, they are unable to keep to time schedules, and slippage seems to grow along an exponential path. By keeping careful track of matters it is at least possible to spot the drift earlier, if not avoid it altogether, and take appropriate action sooner. Of course no device can assist elicitors when they choose to ignore the warning signs of escalating friction; it is as easy in elicitation as in any other field just to carry on in the current direction and hope things work out.

The elicitor should keep track of the process, logging any problems with:

- the knowledge — e.g. complexity or obscurity;
- the expert — inability to articulate, or unwillingness to cooperate;
- the environment — conditions that make communication difficult, e.g. noise or interruptions;
- the elicitation process itself — availability of the expert, or inability to stick to plans;
- spotting drift from the goals of the project's requirement.

Of course many practitioners may already have made it automatic carefully to log the elicitation as it progresses but, as is often the case, many more acknowledge the necessity than those who actually practise it. This is why we recommend building this aspect into the whole approach, so that it becomes habit without significant extra effort. These aspects are then effectively considered alongside all the others.

2.3.7 Some questions about project requirements

The prospective elicitor must have clear objectives, and must be prepared to attend to the following issues:

- What is the ultimate goal of the process? Does this impose any special constraints or requirements?
- What general difficulties have arisen? Or are likely to arise? What would be required to solve them? Could there be problems of scale, timetable, changes in the conditions, change of expert or resourcing difficulties?
- Is the timescale realistic? What happens if more time is required? What has to go if there is no more available?
- What happens if assumptions suddenly change?
- What if major personality conflicts emerge?
- Has everyone been consulted on what is going on? Is the project management adequate?

• What if the expert is not really, or not sufficiently, expert? How easily can another be found? Does the elicitor have a choice of expert?

It may be that some or even none of these questions can be answered by the elicitor. Nevertheless, it may be vital to find out, and find out who does know, in order to assess what difference it will make to the success and timing of the project.

Project requirements are best monitored with the active co-operation of all persons assigned to the project (Mitchell, C., 1989). The expert, who may be better placed to spot a worrying trend, or at least to make comments that might alert the elicitor to one, may make important contributions to project discussions.

The elicitor is a primary member of the project and in order to have some responsibility for the outcome they must state their requirements at the planning stage of a project. This is appropriate and crucial for the success of the project.

Above all, elicitors are authorities in their field of knowledge elicitation, and their views should be given a great deal of credence. Experience still counts when assessing project requirements. Methods are being developed to assist explanation of the elicitation process, which should give more weight to the elicitor's word. But until these are fully in place, elicitors should not be afraid to assert themselves to be heard.

2.4 USING DOMAIN VIEWS

There may be occasions where it is not feasible to structure the information within one of the Domain Views, and for some elicitation tasks, and on very small projects, the expert can talk about their knowledge in a linear fashion. This is especially the case where a particular problem set is the major focus of an expert's activity. The information the expert needs to recall in one problem may require a great deal of information from other areas, and display some necessary interdependencies which make it difficult for the elicitor to follow. However the elicitor may feel that if the expert is confined within a Domain View, valuable material will be lost. Rather than be restrictive, the elicitor then just accepts the information at present, and analyses it later.

If the elicitor had taken too strong a line on what is acceptable at any given stage, and intervenes and restricts the expert too severely, the expert might be forced unwittingly into obscuring some important relationships or interdependencies. These might be lost, and the process becomes protracted by the sheer effort required to keep the expert in the more artificial direction.

These two cases, on the one hand sticking to Domain Views, or on the other, following the natural flow of the knowledge, are in fact the horns of a purely theoretical dilemma. The solution here, as so often in elicitation, is for the practitioner to use judgement. It is largely a question of assessing what consequences will follow given either decision, also it should emerge fairly quickly if the wrong strategy is being pursued. The elicitor should not be ashamed to admit to the expert that a mistake has been made. An explanation of the problem to the expert and an outline of the change in approach is logical, but the elicitor must not vacillate, or chop and change too often. The elicitor must not get caught in the middle of two alternatives otherwise confusion will result.

2.5 FORMULATING QUESTIONS

So far we have dealt with possible Domain Views individually and looked at the kinds of question that each might suggest (Bainbridge, L., 1986; Lehnert, W., 1978). This is useful, especially for the initial, higher level and more general questioning. For later questioning we want increasingly to integrate the growing pattern of knowledge and, at the same time, have a means of generating questions.

Using the categories already selected by the elicitor, each View can be paired in turn with one of the others, so that all possible combinations are tried, and each unique combination reviewed to see if any new aspect of the domain occurs that suggests a question the elicitor should ask of the expert. This process of cross fertilization might bring out further particular questions that the elicitor must consider, or a different approach to the expertise that has not already been considered, and a different line of questioning. This procedure can also be used to provide a check-list, ensuring that all relevant questions and aspects actually have been covered, and that the elicitor's questioning strategy is as complete as possible, ensuring thoroughness, whilst allowing a framework and context within which to seek information.

The examples given below are purely for illustration; in practice many more could be generated, if required, depending on the needs and circumstances of a particular project.

Example

Put each of the domain views against each of the others.

Expert	Knowledge	(1)
	Environment	(2)
	Users	(3)
Knowledge	Environment	(4)
	Users	(5)
Environment	Users	(6)

Clearly there is still some work for the elicitor in thinking carefully about what these different combinations suggest. It cannot work without the application of some mental effort and a minimal exercising of the elicitor's imagination. It is at best a useful means of prompting the elicitor to think about possibilities that might otherwise have been missed.

The degree to which cross-referencing between the Domain Views is necessary will depend on: the degree of complexity displayed in the expertise itself, and the required degree of complexity demanded by the target application for which the knowledge is required. The two may not necessarily be the same. It is the latter that normally determines the complexity and detail (granularity) of the knowledge required and thus determines the depth and sophistication of the questions.

This procedure obviously becomes more cumbersome as the number of domain views increases and some of the questions that occur have already been dealt with, or are not particularly relevant, but it also tends to reveal some of the less obvious ideas and interdependencies.

Some examples from the above combinations might be:

- Are the users' requirements the same as those of the expert? (Expert/Users)
- Do the users possess part of the knowledge? (Knowledge/Users)
- Will some aspects of the environment need to be reproduced in the new system, and could this produce unforeseen problems at a much later stage? (Environment/Requirements)

And so on. The same process can be carried out within a given view, where there are subdivisions. This is particularly useful where:

- one particular view is necessarily larger that the others, for example the domain knowledge usually involves much information,

- one view is more important than another, or
- a view requires a more detailed investigation.

The development of the elicitor's questioning reflects the degree of their sophistication in understanding the expertise so far. By refining their questioning strategy, they will uncover more allowing the probing to go deeper, if necessary, or allowing the whole process to move on to the next area more quickly. This is the same sort of process that characterizes all efficient learning strategies: as we refine our understanding we can ask more penetrating questions. Like learning in any area, however the process requires patience, and tolerance of some mistakes, because they are inevitable, but can frequently teach more than any book or paper about elicitation.

The degree to which this question generation approach is useful depends largely on the willingness of the elicitor to be imaginative and creative (Golan, S., 1963) and follow a more systematic and thorough investigation of possibilities, even if the return on mental investment is sometimes low.

3 The interview

3.1 INTRODUCTION

The interview is still the primary means of acquiring an expert's knowledge for the time being. Efforts such as machine based rule induction (Fox, J., 1984; Hart, 1985) where the expert interacts directly with an expert system, have demonstrated some success in small systems, in terms of ease of development, but largely, where there is any degree of complexity involved, the role of the elicitor as intermediary is still required, and the chances are that there will be a role for some form of interviewing in the process. It is well worth investing some time to investigate the background and dynamics of the process therefore. We recommend several different but integrated techniques of interviewing, specifically adapted to the needs of the elicitor, expert and the type of knowledge being elicited.

The function of the interview is quite specific in knowledge elicitation. Just like the many other techniques recruited from other disciplines to serve their turn in knowledge elicitation, interviewing has been borrowed and adapted to serve the new task. The ease with which interviewing is able to serve the function of eliciting knowledge depends on how thoroughly and how well that process of adaptation has been done. Thus even those who have experience of conducting interviews in other areas cannot necessarily just transfer that experience wholesale and expect instant results in knowledge elicitation.

Practitioners who complain about the inherent problems of interviewing should ensure first that they have looked carefully at the ways it must be adapted to the specific task of elicitation. There are problems with this technique, as there are with any other. In the course of what follows we hope to show how these factors can be identified and minimized. In any case, any inherent problems associated with interviewing as a method are offset by the very significant advantages of the intrinsic power, flexibility and adaptability of interviewing. This is why it is still one of the main techniques in knowledge elicitation and we hope to demonstrate how it can be used to best advantage.

To do so will require two chapters. In the first we look at some of the factors which can make the difference between successful and unsuccessful practice of the technique. The second will detail the nitty gritty aspects of interviewing: the roots of developing transcripts, and the adaptations required specifically for eliciting knowledge.

3.1.1 A word of warning

We must repeat a warning given in the introduction as it is especially relevant here. Throughout the discussion it will be necessary to mention ideas drawn from many disciplines: psychology, social and cognitive science, philosophy and so on, the ideas that we are required to assess are diverse and heterogeneous. Because the focus of our attention is specifically on interviewing, we frequently cannot give each the attention and depth of treatment it deserves. For the sake of the beginner and non-specialist, as much as for the specialist out of their own area, we are required not to assume any specialist training or education and to try and keep the level of information and discussion uniform and relatively uncomplicated. Readers with some specialist training are therefore asked to be patient with any apparently reductive treatment of complex ideas and issues. We have attempted to provide adequate references (given at the end of the book) for the interested reader to follow up.

3.1.2 Function of the interview

We noted above that because the interview as a technique for knowledge elicitation is being adapted to meet the special needs of elicitation we cannot necessarily use the same practices that have been developed elsewhere for a different context. An example will make this clear.

Consider these three different examples of interview situations: interviewing someone for a job; someone under arrest being questioned by the police; and an adoption interview where prospective parents are being examined for their suitability. All of these involve different assumptions and expectations. Usually we might expect less cooperation from the interviewee under arrest, and as arrest is an unwelcome short-term procedure, very little attention will be given to forming a good long-lasting relationship. In the case of a job interview, to enquire too keenly into someone's personal affairs might cause legitimate offence, whereas for the purposes of adoption such details are the essence of the required information, and this interviewing requires a long-term relationship which must prevail for successful adoption to occur and to continue, and so on. Because of these different assumptions we would therefore need to adapt our main use of interviewing method to suit the context.

For elicitation, these methods are: (1) expert focused interviewing, (2) structured interviewing, and (3) 'think aloud' interviewing. Each of these methods is uniquely defined, and an interview is generally of one type. However there are occasions when combinations of other interviewing methods are required in practical interviewing. These issues are discussed in great detail in Chapter 5.

We shall consider in more detail how the requirements of elicitation mould the function of, and hence our approach to, interviewing. This analysis is the more necessary because any lack of clarity about the function and requirements of the interview process will most likely decrease the accuracy of information obtained, and the efficiency of knowledge transfer, and may even threaten the success of the elicitation project altogether.

3.2 CONCERNING THE EXPERT

3.2.1 Preparation — mutual understanding

Good knowledge transfer between the expert and the elicitor requires sound cooperation and mutual understanding. Remember to: (a) consult with the expert and agree what the purpose and scope of each of the interviews is, prior to commencing the interviews; (b) tell the expert what interview methods you will be using, and what therefore you expect in response. If both parties are correctly set for the ensuing interaction there is less likelihood of misunderstanding and the frustration that crossed-purposes can engender. The expert who has been properly briefed and prepared by the elicitor, has had the chance to organize thoughts and is able to respond more easily and comfortably to questioning. The expert is less likely to get irritated or confused if the elicitor is required to interrupt or asks to come back to a specific context, when the interview is drifting because the context and level of detail have been agreed from the start, and the expert knows about the technique the elicitor is using.

3.2.2 Communication factors

It may help a great deal to know how the expert gains knowledge and expertise as this will provide clues for further elicitation (Klodner, J., 1983). The expert may have learned from:

- reading books
- using manuals
- formal instruction
- watching and copying others
- simply being a tutor
- experimenting, testing a hypothesis
- trial and error, learning from mistakes

The expert's learning may have been informal, poor, or lacking a practical component. Later learning and experience may or may not have filled in the gaps left uncovered by experience or formal tuition. Find out about the expert's training background and discuss it if they are willing. This may be a task for the end of a normal session, or during a break, or even outside the elicitation process, if feasible.

There will be enormous variations in the ability of experts to articulate their thinking. An expert without formal training may be entirely unaware of the formal regularities of structure and procedure that exist within the domain knowledge that is manipulated. The expert may have served an apprenticeship under another expert, and acquired knowledge and skill without having to formally understand its basis, even though such knowledge might have been available. Understanding this may help to isolate and overcome many difficulties and potential pitfalls (Miller, G., 1978). Check to see if an interview is the only way of gaining information, and plan well ahead for any areas that will require special equipment, techniques, testing, or personnel. It is so easy to be caught out by overlooking such requirements. What seemed insignificant at the outset, now has increasingly devastating consequences when subsequent plans are wrecked because of it.

It may be, for instance, that one relatively minor part of the expert's job involves a special skill, such as mentally estimating the tension in a set of wires. There is no reason to expect that an expert will be able to describe such a skill verbally (unless the expert has previously had a special reason or interest in so doing). Clearly in such a case the elicitor needs to think in advance of how to discover the basis of this skill of estimation. The elicitor can do this using task analysis (Baume, R., 1983). Task analysis entails the main task be divided into various sub-tasks which can then be treated, as far as possible, as discrete areas for analysis. Information is sought about each of the sub-tasks. The elicitor should take each task in turn, noting the task that precedes it and the one to follow. The elicitor should also identify elements that are shared between sub-tasks, or linked to other larger component tasks, until, eventually, a clear picture of what the expert does is revealed. Perhaps diagrams will be necessary, perhaps a video of the task, or a session involving repertory grid techniques (Eden, C. and Jones, S., 1984) to discover how the expert's qualitative judgements can be emulated in an expert system.

Imagine yourself trying to describe verbally to someone how to play the violin, or rebuild a car engine. Systematic observation will help here, and this might take some careful planning ahead: for the equipment, somewhere suitable to set it up (does the environment condition the task, could a video be used there?). Even more important it may involve a completely different type of task to be able to view, and properly interpret, the result. Will it be obvious, for instance, whether the essential aspects of what the expert does are visually clear, and stand out from say, a great deal of visual information that is accidental? The elicitor may need assistance to help interpret information, or a great deal more time, talking to the expert, to sort out what is essential. Assess the qualitative aspects of the domain and knowledge. What degree of complexity is involved in the expert's performance? The degree of structure in the domain or the knowledge might influence the degree of difficulty in communicating the expertise (Wright, G., 1987). Contrast for example:

• a computer language domain, which is reasonably explicit, well structured, and comparatively well documented, and
• a legal or financial domain, where a great deal of expertise is based on the skill of interpretation, and where much of the domain knowledge and assumptions are implicit.

The law, even though extensively documented, requires a very large body of extensively trained specialists to interpret and enact it. Legal knowledge is more diffuse, heuristic and informal, and may require different and a great deal more skill in communication.

Example

Prediction in weather forecasting has become more reliable with the inception of mathematical and computer modelling techniques. Prediction of horse racing form, and spotting potential winners, is still very much a black art. Yet more or less the same process operates: identifying the important factors, assessing their interdependence, and devising reliable generalizations on which to base a prediction. The difference made by a living thing (the horse) instead of a physical system (the weather) makes a disproportionate difference to the overall degree of difficulty in characterizing the heuristics involved.

Such considerations are bound to affect the techniques employed in elicitation. Mechanical aids such as card (concept) sorting or mathematical modelling might be suitable for testing some of the knowledge in a more structured domain, but not where the domain is less well defined.

Generally it is worth bearing in mind that even an articulate expert is no guarantee of accurate and relevant information. The elicitor must be flexible, and ensure careful verification of information, no matter how articulate and cooperative the expert may be.

3.2.3 The expert's motivation

During the process of elicitation the expert must be kept properly motivated, and this requires thought and consideration from the elicitor (Weinburg, G.). A friendly relationship based on mutual trust may go a long way to ensuring the continuing enthusiasm or at least, cooperation, of the expert. Impatient, impertinent and provocative questioning will be disastrous for the project. The expert is not just a source of knowledge and information, the expert is an active participant, and without willing consent and cooperation little can be achieved. Obvious though it may seem, all too often it is overlooked. Transcript evidence reveals elicitors taking it for granted that the knowledge the expert possesses, often achieved at great personal effort on the part of the expert, is just there for the taking. The elicitor must understand how motivation can be engendered and maintained.

When looking at human motivation it is useful to distinguish between extrinsic and intrinsic motivation:

- Intrinsic motivation is that which arises out of the expert's own internalized reasons or personal interests.
- Extrinsic motivation is any external factor which provides the

expert with sufficient reason to continue to cooperate with the elicitor.

Ideally we would want our expert to be intrinsically motivated, that is, that the expert's motivation should be internal rather than requiring any external prompting. For instance, a working expert system which allowed the hard pressed and busy expert to delegate the less interesting part of a consultancy load on to the system, would free the expert to spend more time on the more interesting or more challenging aspects of the work, which in turn would provide intrinsic motivation. Hence the expert has a personal interest in seeing the system built and would need little convincing that any difficulty in eliciting expertise would be worth the trouble, thus the elicitor's job is made considerably easier. It is possible the expert might become fascinated by the process of knowledge elicitation itself, and this provides the spur that retains enthusiasm.

In practice, however, some form of extrinsic motivation is usually necessary. Intrinsic motivation, even if successfully engendered in the expert, can be brittle. Even where it is present, the elicitor would be unwise to count on it alone to see the process through. Even when things seem to be going well, the elicitor should think of ways to boost the expert's motivation externally, and provide means to enhance the expert's extrinsic motivation.

Removing obstacles to motivation

Technology in general, and expert systems in particular, have suffered because of inflated publicity — fears have been planted by inflated claims, for instance, machines that can think and perform better than human experts. (A few systems can, but they usually emulate only a tiny segment of an expert's total task.) People engaged in the apparently innocent task of constructing useful knowledge based systems which can be shown (eventually) to be beneficial in almost every respect have initially an additional task of removing fears about the technology. Some of these fears are perfectly reasonable: some experts are fearful that what they know may be misused, or that a system will de-value their role or de-skill their job; they might be cynical of any system being able to perform at anywhere near human performance levels, and understandably some people feel, perhaps secretly, rather threatened by such factors.

Most of these fears are generally groundless. Yet expert systems can change the way people work, knowledge they use is available to more people than before and invariably they must change some traditional work patterns.

It is a vital aspect of the elicitor's preparatory work to ensure that the expert, or anyone else directly contributing to the project's development is: reassured about the scope, aims and consequences of participating, and feels comfortable about discussing any matter which they are concerned about. The elicitor should see it as part of the job to find out how the expert feels about the project, whether motivation is good, and if there are any ways in which to give reassurance if it is required.

The elicitor should take these concerns seriously, no matter how groundless they are felt to be. The elicitor should take the trouble to explain clearly what is actually involved. Never underestimate the destructive power of worry and fear. The point is to ensure that everyone understands that the project they are participating in is not destructive or harmful, to them or to others.

Once any legitimate concern has been dealt with, the way is open for providing positive ways of increasing the interest and enthusiasm of the expert, and any other participants. Simple things, like promptness, politeness and efficient organization, obviously help.

Providing motivation

The elicitor should look for any aspect of the elicitation or system building which appears to evoke a positive response or interest, and can provide an opening for the elicitor to engage the expert's interest. This requires that the elicitor is able to read between the lines in discussions with others, and knows how to check responses subtly, reading feedback cues from others responses. The elicitor should provide any information the expert requires, and explain anything that the expert wants to understand, whether or not it is strictly necessary.

To disregard such an interest might result in apathy, frustration or disappointment later, all of which could contribute to a general atmosphere of de-motivation affecting the project as a whole. He/ she should ensure that benefits have been pointed out and, if necessary, explain any that have resulted from the success of the project. Don't assume that they are obvious. It may be that although the result of the project will not directly benefit the expert, the result will help others substantially. This may encourage the expert to make the effort, though not always. Although it is important to make out a positive case for the expert to help others, it is unlikely that making him/her feel guilty about not helping others will provide adequate motivation. More likely the reverse.

The elicitor should point out the possible benefits to the expert of better understanding of knowledge that often results from participating in the elicitation process. The expert may acquire a more explicit model of the knowledge, and may gain valuable new insights into aspects of the work. It is even the case that experts have been helped by the elicitation process to find better methods, or more efficient practices, should they desire them: 'For example, when considering the class of amines, a chemist wrote out 30 interesting amine superatoms which were believed to have exhausted the possibilities. The program (DENDRAL) was convincing in showing that there were in fact 31 possibilities' (Buchanan, B. and Feigenbaum, E., 1977). It may be worth the elicitor pointing to these possibilities as a means of engaging the experts' commitment and enthusiasm, or it may be worth letting experts discover this for themselves.

Interest should be shown in the expert's field. This does not necessarily mean too much prior research of the domain beforehand, but the elicitor must appear to be well motivated when interacting with the expert. An elicitor who comes across as bored, or uninterested in the expert's field will not impress the expert, who has probably spent a great deal of working life and, in all likelihood, a substantial personal investment of effort, to acquire the present high level of expert proficiency.

Experience shows most experts are well motivated and they take a great deal of trouble and effort to explain, to guide and support the elicitor throughout the project. Experts are usually interested in what they do, and they like to see their knowledge and expertise used for some benefit. Experts may become very involved in the development of the system, and will follow any advancement or prototyping with great interest. The expert should become a partner in the project and work with the elicitor (and any others) as a team.

3.2.4 The expert's personality

Given that the elicitor is working with a human source of expertise, and knowing that expertise is an integral part of their personality, an elicitor should look at the influences that human personality can have on the process of elicitation (Watzlawick, P., 1964; Smith, N., 1968; Kounin, J., 1941).

The expert's personal characteristics

How does the expert cope with stress or ambiguity? Furthermore, how do different aspects of the project affect participants? For instance:

- is the expert honest about mistakes?
- have preferred ways of expressing things?
- feel comfortable with numerical data?
- prefer using analogies?

And so on.

The above only mentions a few of the many possibilities. The others will depend on the circumstances and personalities with which the elicitor is engaged.

The elicitor should be aware of the way these factors affect the performance of the expert, as they can make a considerable difference to the ease and speed with which information transfer is carried out. The discussion below will look further at the effects of personality, and what can be done to accommodate it during the elicitation.

Preparing the expert

How well you prepare, inform, orientate, and involve the expert will make a difference to his or her response. The expert is sacrificing time and effort to reveal knowledge. If you are well prepared and efficient, it will go some way to reassuring the expert, inspiring confidence and enhancing motivation. Certainly involving the expert in the process, explaining the overall aims, procedures and keeping the expert informed at each stage of the process will help to keep up personal (intrinsic) motivation. The more an expert can be encouraged to identify the more likely there will be a good fast flow of high quality information.

- always ensure that your preparation is thorough and adequate. Have you really thought it through?
- Continually re-assess your plans. Does what you have in mind still seem to fit with what you know of the expert you are working with?
- Have you taken enough trouble to ensure that the expert feels comfortable with the environment for elicitation from the outset?
- Have you planned for reasonable breaks between interviews in

your timetable? Are they flexible and realistic, or will the first interruption of your plan sink it without trace?
• Have you got all the props and back-up materials you need? Including the mundane ones: enough paper, spare pens or pencils and so on.

Novice elicitors should bear in mind that generally it is rare to overdo preparation, but very easy to do too little. It is also essential to think carefully about the quality of preparatory effort; a great deal of time and effort may be wasted by preparation that is not relevant to the actual circumstances of a particular project.

The effects of stress

There is little point in pushing on with a session if the expert is over-tired. There is even less point in starting a new session if the expert is ill or too preoccupied with something else. Look out for symptoms that your expert is under duress:

• fatigue
• apathy
• excessive restlessness
• sudden mood swings and irritability
• loss of concentration
• careless mistakes

Is the cause:

• the elicitation process itself?
• your elicitation techniques?
• something outside (family for instance)?
• contract or management constraints of some kind?

The cause may be difficult to find out — certainly tact and diplomacy will be essential — but to ignore such symptoms may be disastrous. It could be that the expert is having to cope with the full pressure of a normal workload, in addition to the added burden of elicitation, itself a tiring process. Attempting to get some of the load taken from the expert will not only be of assistance, it could assist the efficiency of the elicitation. If no reduction of the workload is possible, could the elicitation sessions be shortened? Could shorter sessions re-scheduled over a longer period help alleviate stress for example?

Fears can also cause stress (Selye, H., 1952). Fears of expert system technology degrading or de-skilling jobs, worries about intrusion into the expert's personal knowledge (Shaw, M. L. G.), even the fear that experts may have less knowledge than they originally thought, or that it is less worthwhile than they thought. Irrational worries and fears may not be well founded, seem unjustified, or exaggerated, but they are nevertheless common to most people and make a difference to the way we behave, especially under pressure. Regardless of whether it seems justified to us, it is quite common for an expert to be worried, even to feel threatened by the elicitation, and therefore to feel under pressure and experience stress. The elicitor's skill at handling people is therefore crucial.

An expert who is under excessive stress can have a dramatic adverse effect on the elicitation process. It can affect the expert's ability to cope with questioning, the quality and quantity of the answers, the ease with which information is recalled, the extent and accuracy of the expert's articulation, judgements and, more generally, the success of your relationship with the expert. Any trouble you take to overcome such difficulties will assist the process, most likely enhance the expert's motivation, and build a better working bond between you and the expert.

- Consult the expert about your requirements, goals and plans.
- Allow the expert to assist in the control of the process.
- Make sure you know about the constraints and pressures on the expert.
- If there are signs of excessive stress, take any immediate positive action possible to relieve it.

3.3 CONCERNING THE ELICITOR

3.3.1 The role of the elicitor

The elicitor needs to develop skill in analysing the interaction with the expert both during and after the interview. The elicitor needs to be able to adapt to the personality of the interviewee, sometimes subordinating their own wishes and needs to maintain a smooth running interaction. The elicitor must be following the process of the interview at two levels simultaneously, they must: (1) follow the dialogue with the expert on the knowledge, and (2) be aware of the personal feedback signals that are coming from the expert. The elicitor should be able to gauge what effect the questions and probings are having, by reading the expert's feedback of cues of movement, gesture and expression in face and voice. This requires skill and practice, but we believe that it can be learnt [see Section 3.3.8 below: How Can Elicitation Skills Be Learned?].

The process of successful interviewing is dependent on successfully reading the feedback from the interviewee. It is not necessary to be a mind reader, merely to increase your awareness and sensitivity to the many clues and signals that each of us give when we communicate. Most people have some level of ability in reading these response signals from others, the object for the elicitor is to become more conscious of them.

The elicitor must develop a conscious set (method of feedback) to notice and interpret personal feedback during elicitation sessions. Initially this will probably make the elicitor very uncomfortable; — it seems very strained and artificial — but with some practice it becomes second nature, providing the elicitor doesn't give up through fear, impatience, or pressure from others.

As far as is realistic, interviews should be made as pleasant as possible (though they must remain business like and formal to a certain extent). The elicitor should ensure plans have been made for regular refreshment breaks, these are a necessity not a luxury if efficient exchange of information is to be maintained. Attempts should be made to form a friendly, or at least good humoured, relationship with the expert, showing proper consideration for the expert's feelings or mood, but maintaining control of the process, and being positively assertive if necessary.

It is very easy for an interview to wander away from the point, and quite difficult politely to interrupt someone when they are already mentally set to talk along one particular line. But it is a necessary skill, and again, can be learnt [see Section 3.3.8 below: How Can Elicitation Skills Be Learned?].

Positively acknowledge the expert's time away from the usual task. This the elicitor can do by:

• being punctual at the interviews
• being thoroughly prepared
• making the interviews as smooth running and pleasant as possible
• making the best use of the time available.

Positive acknowledgement of the expert's extra workload will more likely assist in getting results. Knowledge elicitation can be an extremely tiring process, managers should be made aware of this fact, as well as the importance of good estimation and planning so the expert knows how much time will be spent in elicitation sessions.

The elicitor should not complain or grumble about any difficulties occurring as this will most likely result in the expert losing confidence. Relate any difficulties to a specific aspect of the knowledge or task where it is the concern of the expert or the domain; if the problem is concerned with some matter outside, then it would be more business-like not to raise it in an interview unless essential, but wait until it can be dealt with by the person it actually concerns.

What makes a good elicitor?

A good elicitor should know how to remain patient above all. Patience will be required in the intermediary stages especially when the learning curve is at its highest and when much of the knowledge is still unclear or unknown.

Patience will be required with your own efforts as the elicitor, and also with experts if they are unfamiliar with the elicitation process. The ability to control feelings of rising panic, which may occur as a result of the slow development of understanding, would be an asset.

The elicitor should have the ability to analyse a situation as a detached observer would. This enables the elicitor to predict and judge projects as they develop without becoming immersed in trivia or succumbing to the cumulative affects of pressure associated with learning in an unfamiliar situation.

It is an advantage to like people and to share an interest in their work. Try to interact naturally, but also in a businesslike, task-oriented way.

Knowing something about human cognition may be an advantage, knowing the limits and characteristics of memory and attention spans could prevent the elicitor from expecting unreasonable results from elicitation. But formal knowledge is not a pre-requisite whereas some sensitivity to the feelings of others is.

3.3.2 Learning constructive control

The novice elicitor should try to develop the skills for dealing with people, or extend those already gained. Anyone engaged in interviewing others, even if only with formal techniques, requires a minimum competence in this respect. Skill in handling interaction with others is beginning to receive recognition now as a legitimate and important concern in knowledge acquisition. Anyone interacting with others, but especially those who do so on a professional basis, must develop a feeling for communicating fluently with others beyond the level of ordinary social interaction. Try and overcome any feelings that consciously learning communication skills is unnecessary, manipulative or an affection. As far as the elicitor is concerned, working with others to gain information is the essence of the job, and the ability to communicate easily and well is of paramount importance, for the sake of all those working on the project.

There are now courses available and some literature has been published on these matters (Carnegie, D., 1981). While there is obviously no substitute for real-life experience, skills such as diplomacy and tact, correct self-assertion and the ability to listen, can be learned up to a point. It is foolish merely to assume that all these things come automatically. Everybody thinks they're good at people skills (and knows most others are not) but there are few who could not improve.

Action

- Get feedback from the expert on your handling of the process. Allow some means of commenting on the current elicitation practices and ask for suggestions and constructive criticism.
- Investigate the possibility of training people who will be frequently involved with knowledge elicitation projects. Is it possible to set up a mechanism for passing on previous experience?
- Try to become conscious of yourself, as elicitor, in action. Listen to tape recordings of interviews. At first it will seem awkward and irritating, but, with patience and practice, you can use it to enhance your performance.

3.3.3 Controlling interview direction

During an interview, there is a need to exercise implicit rather than explicit control. The more the elicitor has thought out, prepared, planned, decided what knowledge is required and is discussed in the elicitation session, the less likely it will be that explicit interventions are needed when the interview is in progress. To ensure the interview does not drift off course the elicitor must direct the flow, avoid regressions and continually guide the discussion back to the subject. Planning must include sufficient flexibility to allow for the unexpected, and the necessity of revised direction, or coping with additional and unforeseen material, and so on. The elicitor should clearly signal all intentions and requirements to the expert, both before and, where necessary, during the interview. This is part of the process of getting appropriate feedback, both about the process of information capture itself and, indirectly, the insights into the expert's feelings gauged from the responses.

3.3.4 Relevance

Limits need to be set as to what comments or responses are relevant. Considering the cost per hour of tape, the work time taken up in interviews, and the further time and cost of transcription, the expert and elicitor's time is precious. Controlling the content of the interview successfully means there will be little irrelevant material in the transcripts, which in turn requires a disciplined approach during interviews. Transcribing a tape full of incidental information and chatter is frustrating and time wasting. There should be enough time during breaks for casual talk about other matters. That is the time to participate in repartee and relaxation. Controlling the boundaries of the interview from the outset, together with clear signals from the elicitor, help to indicate to the expert what the elicitor regards as irrelevant information. An expert who is clear about what to expect and what constitutes a relevant response is far less likely to interfere with the professional quality of the interview.

3.3.5 Consideration

Control must be balanced with consideration. The elicitor must also learn to use judgement to ensure that any intrusion does not threaten the process. Interrupting unnecessarily may inhibit the expert. The idea of effective control implies consideration and empathy. It is therefore part of the elicitor's responsibility to be aware of any contribution made and the effect it has on others. Our experience shows that lack of self-awareness can cause problems directly. Antagonism can quickly delay or destroy effective exchange. If you are not communicating effectively is it partly your own fault? It is not always possible to keep changing the expert because you cannot seem to get on with them, or get the kind of knowledge that you want from them. Without becoming over-conscious, the elicitor should engage in some self-analysis, and honestly assess any shortcomings. This can provide valuable feedback for improved future performance. Bring the expert into all important decisions which will directly affect him or her: the length of sessions, frequency of breaks, time-tabling, setting and so on. The more clear the expert is about the process, the less likely unforeseen problems induced by stress, worry or antagonism will come into play.

3.3.6 Listening

The elicitor must be able to listen actively. There is an important distinction to be made between listening attentively and merely hearing. The difference is essentially one of degree of attention and concentration, and the habit of using what is heard to feedback accurate and appropriate responses, as quickly as the interview demands, to keep it moving efficiently and in the right direction.

Most of the content of a transcript should be from the expert. The elicitor must also be able to keep silent and listen at appropriate times. This is frequently more effective in eliciting knowledge than asking a stream of questions, especially in the orientation stage of knowledge elicitation.

Before elicitors can usefully contribute questions that penetrate through to the information needed, they must gain a feeling for the domain (Sowa, F., 1984). This requires attentive listening. The elicitor already understands enough about the expert's knowledge and task, and need only interrupt occasionally. The most active period for the elicitor occurs when probing for in-depth information, during the structured interviews. Even then, succinct formulation of questions is still desirable, and the transcript should be predominantly the words of the expert. The ability to listen attentively is a skill that can be developed.

3.3.7 Talking

Novice elicitors are often over-talkative. This may lower the expert's concentration. Talking too much about the direction of the interview while it is taking place can be inhibiting, even (inadvertently) misleading. The expert gets confused, and begins to answer what he/she thinks the elicitor wants to hear, not what is actually important about practical behaviour, so that the expert no longer relates what is actually done, but instead becomes enslaved by the elicitor's line of thought. The elicitor, though apparently staying in control, can no longer understand how the expert thinks, what the domain priorities are, or how strategies are implemented, let alone discovering any other useful information.

The expert may be irritated by interruptions and quite naturally feels that the knowledge disclosed is important, and has not been given the opportunity to express it in the way that is natural. Time may be scarce and expensive, and the expert is unlikely to relish the prospect of undergoing lengthy inquisitions.

3.3.8 How can elicitation skills be learned?

What is the best method to learn (or teach) personal and control skills? The elicitor can learn such skills, or teach what they know already, by organizing and participating in simulation exercises with other colleagues. Role playing games and interview simulations are invaluable for increasing sensitivity and awareness. Being on the receiving end of the elicitation process can be very enlightening, even though the elicitor is not under the pressure of a real interview. The participants can:

- identify faults, yours and of others, thus increasing awareness of what can go wrong;
- collectively discuss solutions to common problems, and the chance to compare notes, based on real experience;
- quicken the process of learning from experience, and allow the participants the invaluable luxury of making mistakes and learning from them without paying the penalty that might be incurred in a real interview;
- provide a realistic arena for testing new ideas and techniques;
- increase confidence, especially for beginners, in a naturalistic way;
- obtain direct feedback, and helpful comments from more sympathetic listeners who are prepared to go into more depth in analysing someone's performance.

These exercises can provide a key component in the development of skill in knowledge elicitation. Obviously valuable as a training exercise for beginners, it can go on being useful even for the most seasoned professional if the elicitor is prepared to make a modest investment of imagination and is prepared to experiment. It is hard to believe there is anyone practising in this field who could not learn something new from such a scheme.

3.3.9 Observation skills

There are many popular systems for understanding non-verbal and verbal behaviour. In addition to the wealth of literature on formal psychology, there are now methods, often growing out of business and management, which claim to put the task of reading interpersonal behaviour on a systematic and objective foundation. Examples are: Transactional Analysis, Neuro-Linguistic Programming and the growing wealth of literature on so-called 'body language' (Pease, A., 1981).

We do not intend to discuss or recommend any of these systems as there is abundant literature already available and the practitioner must decide whether it is of any use: caveat emptor.

There is, however, a more mundane and commonsense level at which observation skills (Milkaski, R. and Stepp, R., 1983) are relevant. We have already discussed the conscious development of the skill of reading facial or body movements, and verbal cues above (Section 3.3.1). However this must be used with care, such signals are usually bound and determined by a particular context, and are mixed with significant idiosyncratic aspects. The elicitor must be on guard against too simplistic mapping of gesture to interpretation. All we are suggesting here is that the elicitor should set himself to become more aware of these processes. Observing someone's habits of speaking and moving may provide clues both for monitoring the progress of the elicitation session and the effectiveness of the elicitor's questions. In addition the elicitor may be able to spot characteristic signs, in the case of an individual, which tell when a good understanding is getting close and when the trail is lost. For instance, the expert may become enthusiastic when the interview is going well, indicated by leaning forward slightly, gesturing more animatedly or smiling more. Alternatively the expert may indicate discontent: increased restlessness, looking out of the window, or at a watch, or more obvious signs of discomfort like repeated yawning, finger or pencil tapping and so on.

The danger lies in our interpreting restlessness as increased animation for example, and thus misreading discontent as success. This is why we advocate a cautious approach to reading behaviour. Obviously such evanescent signals can only be used as indicators, everything must be checked objectively as far as possible. Such signals remain only an informal guide, though frequently useful they are potentially misleading. Notwithstanding these cautions, personal feedback can be a powerful tool if treated sensibly.

3.3.10 The elicitor's role

The elicitor should attempt to be disinterested (as opposed to uninterested) and unobtrusive at first, and, until ready to probe deeper, allow the expert to do most of the talking. The elicitor steers the process subtly using feedback, and will attempt not to be judgemental, over-critical or impatient, in order to ensure that the expert's sensitivities are not threatened and no resistance to the process triggered (Duncan, S., 1977; Lyle, J., 1989; Downes, C., 1980). The model of a therapist might suggest a better model than thinking of the expert as a problem to be engineered, or as a database knowledge source. Yet just such mistakes are apparent from transcripts.

Absolute beginners

Indeed, analysis of beginner's transcripts reveal that these things are often done. The expert is treated with impatience, especially when questions are not answered specifically or fully. Half page questions from the novice elicitor are followed by one sentence answers from the expert or, worse, just yes/no answers. The expert is now allowed to give information but is reduced to the role of merely confirming a developing model in the head of the elicitor. However this model is not visible since it is not based on the explicit transcripts of the expert's answers, and therefore cannot be cross-checked, by the expert or anyone else, for accuracy, completeness and clarity.

Similarly, it is not unusual to find that beginners just assume that the expert is obliged to cooperate, and must therefore put up with being interrogated. They seem to expect the expert to deliver information. This is arrogant. It is as absurd as believing that one can insert a floppy disk into the expert's head, issue a copy command and extract the expertise complete. Failure to recognize the necessary interactive skills, and prepare for their practice will at best prove costly, at worst could result in failure of a project.

Time and again transcripts reveal the elicitor becoming impatient. If someone cannot live with and tolerate uncertainty, they are unlikely to make a good elicitor. It takes time — and above all patience — for the full picture of the expertise to emerge. Until it does the elicitor must be able to live with incomplete understanding and partial insights. Harassing the expert is unlikely to enhance the process, yet people do this. In knowledge elicitation, patience, tolerance and clear objectives are the key virtues.

Temperament

Patience is different in kind to the things we have been discussing above. When the elicitor is interacting with the expert, constantly receiving unfamiliar information, it is difficult at first to discriminate the essential from the accidental, and assign significance to the parts that will most help to organize some understanding of the domain quickly. It follows that for much of the process the elicitor will not understand, or only partially understand, how the expert performs in the domain. This can be immensely frustrating. Impatience can cost the elicitor dear, by giving way to the impulses that it promotes. Of course, patience cannot be taught. There is little that can be done to improve your patience quota. It is one of several qualities (tolerance, intelligence and so on) that are largely a matter of character and temperament. By being aware of it as a factor, its effects, and your own strengths and weaknesses, you can provide a useful basis for anticipating and avoiding the worst consequences of such problems.

3.4 COGNITIVE FACTORS

3.4.1 Individual differences

Our route to knowledge is mostly dependent on a human agent with a personality and feelings which must be considered if we wish to avoid problems. While most agree this should be considered, little or no effort is really given to working out, in any detail, what the implications are for practical knowledge elicitation. The focus is often so strongly on 'knowledge' as an object in itself, it is sometimes taken for granted that the expert will deliver. The performance of the expert's practice will be informed by habits (Tversky, A. and Kahneman, D., 1974), individual practices, and idiosyncratic ways of perceiving and assessing problems. Though obviously these aspects are seldom entirely idiosyncratic, experts can agree, cooperate and understand one another.

Expert knowledge can be seen as public only in the sense that experts, when practising their skill, should be able both to provide an answer, and give a reasonable explanation for their conclusions. Expert knowledge is also personal in a different sense: that the practice of an expert's skill, because it required a personal investment of effort and learning to create it, means also that all the expert's knowledge is filtered through that particular person's cognitive equipment. So knowledge in general, when mediated through a human expert, is subject to the significant effects of individual differences and the individual's formative experience:

general education, the methods through which the experts learned their skill, and so on.

Most experts practice their skill from experience based on learning the hard way; by trial and error, informed guesswork or the advice and teaching of a predecessor. Even where the domain is bounded by theory, there may be significant advantages in understanding how the expert puts flesh on the dry bones of book knowledge, especially in the context of a practical execution of some task, or in solving some problem in the domain.

3.4.2. Misunderstanding

We do not perceive passively. Our minds are constantly active in constructing patterns and meaningful wholes out of our experience (Rumblehart, G., 1980). It is easy to construct a credible but wrong picture of the emerging knowledge. The elicitor must therefore be patient and thorough. If the elicitor is too hasty, valuable time may be lost by having to go back over parts not completed properly, or inaccurately. There are different ways that information can be misunderstood.

Incompleteness

The first and most obvious type of misunderstanding occurs when the elicitor's information is insufficient or incomplete, a rule for instance, is understood by the elicitor to be more general than it actually is. The expert may have omitted to mention vital details about exceptions, which could cast other important parts of the knowledge, or even the whole of it, into a different perspective.

It is common, for instance, that the expert's normal working environment triggers the expert's recollection during the performance of a task. If it has not been possible to carry out the elicitation in that environment, or to provide essential props used by the expert, failure to recall just this kind of qualifying information may occur. It might be some time before this omission is found and corrected, by which time considerable problems have stacked up unseen.

Incorrect information

The second form of misunderstanding involves false information. Without question, experts rarely mislead deliberately. The expert gives information in good faith, but for a variety of reasons it turns out to be wrong. This may seem odd at first. How can experts be experts and yet have false beliefs about their own knowledge? It is quite possible for someone to practise a skill successfully, using their first order knowledge of how it is done, without them knowing anything about why they are successful or the actual basis of their practice. A good example of this is acupuncture, the techniques of which have been practised for centuries and some of the claims, such as its use for anaesthesia, have been independently verified by western medicine. Yet no explanation for its success is universally accepted. A great deal of medical practice in previous ages was probably based on wrong or misleading assumptions and explanations or beliefs. But where it was effective, it no doubt brought real relief to the sufferer, and kudos to the practitioner.

Misconceptions

The third source of misunderstanding is also the most insidious. It may be the case that both the expert and the elicitor are satisfied that they understand the information they have together uncovered, and both believe that it is complete and accurate. Sometimes even when the expert and elicitor receive the same information about some problem, they may not interpret it in the same way and, in both a metaphorical and literal sense, they may not see the same thing (Stevens, et al.). This is not the same as perceptual distortion or error: neither party's perceptions are actually wrong, neither are being fooled by some lacuna or blind spot of the senses, each has a genuinely different view, or gestalt, of the same information. However, it may not occur to them to check that their separate understandings are similar.

It would be quite possible, for instance, to imagine a situation where someone attempting to elicit information from an expert, even given the right information, constructed it into a different mental schema (Schank, A., et al.) from that intended by the expert. This kind of misunderstanding is quite common in learning contexts, including knowledge elicitation. Part of the role of a teacher is to correct a student's misconceptions. But in the case of knowledge elicitation, there is no 'teacher' role as such, the expert and elicitor are engaged more in a mutual exploration because the expert most likely does not have a conscious model of the knowledge. The dangers of the elicitor misunderstanding in effect, are therefore that much greater. It is crucial for the elicitor to test all conclusions and constantly refer back to the expert for verification of the analysis. It is as important when the elicitor thinks understanding has been reached as when the expert thinks there is a problem. The difficulty lies in discovering that the elicitor's interpretation is a misconception precisely because experts seldom have an explicit model (Schrieber, G., et al. 1988) of their own knowledge and may not be in a position to point out faults. In fact the expert may even be convinced that what the elicitor has revealed is an accurate representation, at least until some critical case reveals otherwise.

The misunderstanding might involve the whole or just a part of the information. The extent of it will undoubtedly affect how costly the misunderstanding proves in time and effort. The effect of even a small misunderstanding can ripple through the whole knowledge model, and we have already had occasion to note the damaging effect that premature extrapolation of incorrect assumptions can have on the following stages of knowledge elicitation and refinement and, later still, on the system development itself.

3.4.3 Other forms of error

Bias

It is possible for the elicitor to distort the expert's knowledge because of biases caused by his or her own strong ideas or assumptions. Dominant ideas which distort the elicitor's thinking, such as common sense assumptions about the world, may not apply, or not in the same way, within the narrow and special limits of the expert's particular domain.

For example, in everyday terms, commonsense notions about colour are entirely sufficient to describe and act on the experiential world. It is unnecessary to think in terms of optical physics to see the world as we normally do. In the domain of optics, the naive everyday model of colour is of no value, and must give way to expert conceptions of light wavelengths.

If the elicitor were to confuse the descriptions given by the expert, and integrate commonsense assumptions (McCarthy, J., 1958) we would say that this had introduced naive bias into the knowledge model. Generally, commonsense perceptions are powerful (because useful) abstractions, and are sometimes difficult to escape from or dislodge (Bouchon, B., and Yager, R., 1986). The idea, for instance, that the sun orbited the earth still seems intuitively plausible, even though we now know the reverse is actually the case.

It is possible that the elicitor may be forced to update an understanding of the expert's knowledge several times in the course of the elicitation process. The more complex the domain or expert task, the more likely this is. Because the elicitor's understanding must be constructed on the basis of what is already known, the chances are fairly great of the knowledge being influenced by currently held ideas and assumptions.

Expectation and pre-conceptions

It is similarly possible to distort information by unwittingly allowing false expectation to shape our perceptions. The human mind is able to complete patterns out of very limited, noisy or incomplete data. Elicitors must be constantly aware of what their expectations are.

It is extremely easy to do violence to incoming information by inadvertently distorting it to fit with the elicitor's pre-existent schemas, already well developed and strong, polarizing new ideas into a form that fits prior expectations and pre-conceptions.

As an elicitor's understanding of the expertise begins to grow, as does their confidence, they risk falling into the trap of allowing their expectations to get in the way of what is actually the case. This is another form of bias, where the elicitor substitutes a set of expectations based on what they have learned so far, instead of correctly interpreting the information that the expert actually gave.

Even though a wrong interpretation may be at odds with the expert's perceptions, we may fail to notice this, preferring to rely on our own interpretation, which we understand better, rather than those which actually matter more, those of the expert. The elicitor is not well placed to judge the significance of what is learned initially, and is liable to construct some other interpretation until a reliable structure has been established between the expert and elicitor.

Prior research into the domain, for instance, may influence the elicitor's perception of what the expert is saying. It could give the elicitor false confidence, which then leads to inattentiveness, thus allowing minute distinctions, which significantly shape the knowledge, to be missed.

Awareness

Misunderstandings between the elicitor and expert because of incomplete information is an important source of error. The elicitor should keep it in mind while involved in or reviewing a session or project. It is often not obvious what the scope of an expert's pronouncements are, and there is no reason to expect unfailing explicit, precise and complete expertise, or even that the expert can provide this. The elicitor should consciously practise reviewing transcripts for their completeness, devising tests to check this. The elicitor may also use intuition, but this cannot be relied on, especially in cases where the missing information does not seem to violate the logic of the rest. As we have already observed, testing and checking are always the bottom line.

As a general guide-line we would be better off assuming that misunderstanding is a lot easier, and more likely, than understanding. Even if this is not true it is more likely to instil the necessary caution when attempting to understand and interpret the expert's knowledge.

3.4.4 Recall

Human recall is not always well organized, linear or consistent, even in experts. It will depend on the circumstances, such as the degree of variance from the expert's normal environment; the extent to which the expert feels comfortable with the process of elicitation; has confidence in the elicitor and so on. The elicitor must therefore learn to be patient during the interview.

Recall is assisted by preparing the expert for the subject area and interviewing technique to be used. With this kind of mental set, even if the proposed content is only decided a short time before the interview, the expert has the opportunity to prepare thinking and activate the mind and the necessary familiar pathways in memory will be easily keyed in to answer questions (Nisbett, R., 1974, 1977). Use the end of the interview for final recall. Leave five minutes at the end of the interview for any additional information or qualifications. With the end in sight the expert may relax more and suddenly provide a great deal of useful information. Important qualifications and reservations will be brought out about what has been said, for instance saying what actually happens rather than what should, sometimes even contradicting previous assertions. It is worth allowing around five to ten minutes after the formal session has finished to allow the expert to relax and collect last thoughts. This last informal phase can prove invaluable.

3.4.5 Validating the information elicited

The elicitor should check and validate all information elicited. Check that:

- your understanding is the same as the expert's;
- you have captured the subtlety of relationships and dependencies;
- all the information is self-consistent and suitably complete for the stage of elicitation;
- you have understood the technical language used;
- the area covered was completed at the level intended;
- there were no important variations or special circumstances to the information.

This can be done in cooperation with the expert, but (a) it is sometimes necessary, depending on the context, to get independent corroboration, (b) devise some tests to check the expert's actual behaviour against what is believed to be the case, (c) an elicitor must also be aware of processes like rationalization. For instance, an expert may provide a perfectly plausible explanation for a behaviour, which, although given in good faith, turns out to be wrong. Or the situation where the expert reveals new aspects of the work which seem to contradict previously established conclusions or, at least, substantially modify them.

The elicitor should expect that recalled information may be less than pure. Cross-checking and validation with another expert may be useful. Is there another expert to assist validation? The elicitor can then comment back to the expert at the next session if there are any apparent anomalies, inconsistencies or problems. Work out consequences from the information given and then put these to the test. Both the inferences and the test will be determined by context. The expert can be given these test cases and problems to work through, and the elicitor can cross-check against the expectations developed in the course of the previous sessions. Reversing roles, the expert often tests the elicitor in solving a problem, watched by the expert. This can be a revealing process, but only if the test has real value and is not done solely to amuse the expert. Ensure that high level aspects are correct:

1. Sequencing of problem solving strategies;
2. Scheduling of tasks;
3. Priority for essential information.

3.5 EXPERT HEURISTICS

'HEURISTIC *a & n*) 1. (a) *Serving to discover; (of computer problem solving) proceeding by trial and error;* ~ *IC METHOD, system of education*

under which the pupil is trained to find out things for himself; hence ~ ICS (n.pl.). 2(n) (Science of) heuristic procedure. [irreg. f.EX heuristics find; . . .]'
Quoted from: *The Concise Oxford Dictionary,* 7th edition.

Among many expert systems communities the most common folk definition of 'heuristics' seems to be 'rule of thumb'. In the absence of regular, tried and tested rules, it is still possible for experts in a domain to perform with a great deal of confidence. The generalizations they use are derived from experience, which form the basis on which they make reliable judgements (Clancey, W., 1986). Often expert knowledge based on heuristic rules requires that the expert understand exception cases which are quite complex and sophisticated. Experts learn to work with uncertain and incomplete information, proceeding on the basis of what works.

3.5.1 Schemas

The importance of the expert's experience is crucial in this process. In the course of learning expertise in a given area, the expert constructs regular mental routines based on repeated practice which are compressed into non-conscious sub-routines, referred to as schemas.

Schemas are analogous in function to computer sub-routines, though far more powerful and flexible (Young, G., 1982). Such schemas become so familiar through repeated use, the expert seems to be working automatically, allowing concentration on variations and differences in the information, rather than having to assess all of it anew in each task or problem.

3.5.2 Problem characteristics versus variant features

Thus, for example, an expert who is asked to estimate the time some operation will take, for planning purposes say, might consider two types of information:

Strategy 1. The specific features of this particular estimation problem.

or

Strategy 2. Estimating on the basis of the variant features, that is, those aspects that emerge as significantly different in comparison with other similar cases.

The first strategy relied on the characteristics of the problem itself viewed in isolation. The second projects the problem against a background of other similar cases and concentrates on the vital points of difference between this and the other cases. Strategy 1 is much more likely to be used by inexperienced problem solvers, making their answers slower and less reliable. Strategy 2 is the expert able to assess patterns of information and isolate only those aspects that matter.

Example

When asked to estimate how long a process would take given various conditions, the expert will add a general overview of factors affecting time estimates in this type of case, and will most likely know which factors, in any particular case, will influence the time-scale. More reasonable time estimates can be obtained by asking the question: How long do projects in this area usually last? (distributional case), (Kahneman, D. and Tversky, A., 1972), rather than the question: What are the specific factors and difficulties that operate in this particular problem? (singular case).

Problem

The expert's increased efficiency is the cause of the elicitor's problems. It is precisely because the expert often does not need to hold crucial parts of knowledge consciously that the description does not follow exactly what is done. Because the patterns of experience have become efficient non-conscious schemas, they are no longer so easy to isolate and make explicit for system design purposes.

This, then, is the challenge of knowledge elicitation: to uncover the pathways of successful expert performance by revealing the submerged knowledge and procedures that the expert has developed in the course of acquiring the skill. Of course simple cases exist where elicitation is relatively straightforward. It may not always be the case that there will be a submerged component, or even that this knowledge is useful or necessary. In many, if not most, of the more sophisticated domains, however, it will be a significant factor.

3.5.3 The role of non-conscious thought

We use the term 'non-conscious thought' for mental processes that are beyond our conscious awareness and direct control. However ugly or clumsy it might seem, we choose this term rather than 'unconscious' or 'sub-conscious' because of possibly misleading associations: we are *not* concerned with the unconscious as a potential repository for psychosis, or the home of archetypes, ESP, dreams or visions. These things may or may not exist in areas outside of our normal awareness, but that is emphatically not our concern here. We simply require a term to indicate that some, perhaps much, mental work proceeds outside of our conscious awareness, allowing us to perform tasks and solve problems based on processes which we are not always directly aware of. To give a trivial illustration: it is often possible to carry out routine and repetitive tasks without conscious thought. One need only to watch someone engaged in trivial conversation, following the story line of a play on television and knitting at the same time.

We noted above that this encoding of experience into non-conscious schemas allows the expert to see tasks and problems in a different way from the novice. It provides the expert with a mental reference grid with which to analyse and classify experience dynamically, discriminating variant factors more likely to affect a solution, enabling the expert to arrive at it more quickly and efficiently. Since it is not easy to access and analyse this reference grid, we must use indirect means correctly to identify and make explicit these schemas. One way we do this is by trying to define characteristic heuristic 'rules' from the evidence of statements and behaviour given by the expert making an explicit representation of the expertise.

Let us now examine the nature of heuristics in more depth.

3.5.4 Characterizing heuristics

As the dictionary definition given above suggests, heuristics are a common behaviour strategy in human affairs, not just the prerogative of experts. Anything which guides our actions in indeterminate situations can be characterized as a heuristic, that is, any situation where we are faced with making a decision with insufficient information, and can devise a guide-line, possibly conditional, for interpreting those circumstances and arriving at some reliable conclusion or judgement. A good illustration of the process lies in proverbs and sayings; like the famous old English proverb that was supposed to have guided shepherds before reliable weather forecasting: 'red sky at night, shepherd's delight, red sky in the morning, shepherd's warning'.

In social situations we are constantly confronted with making decisions about people, whether for instance we can trust them, and we learn fairly early in life that appearances can be deceptive. With increasing social experience, we develop (hopefully) more and more adequate and sophisticated intuitions about people, often based on subtle interactive verbal, facial and physical clues. This is all made necessary because of the near certainty of not having enough information about the person we are dealing with, or at least, not the right information.

Thus we attempt to use reliable social heuristics as a basis for personal judgement, some of which we have received during the course of our education, some based on our own experience, most probably built up from a mixture of both. (Some people's perceptions will remain blocked in certain situations despite these intuitions.)

Likewise, more generally, we learn to estimate, judge probabilities, learn about causal patterns, transfer from similar cases, construct likely scenarios and develop explanations. We assess new experience in a more or less expert way, judging the degree of parallelism, the similarity and difference with our previous experience. Factors which stand out as being new and different then become the focus of attention. The more we can restrict the area in which we have to think about, the narrower and more well defined the 'domain', the better our chances of avoiding confusion and coming to an accurate decision as quickly as possible are likely to be. The heuristic does not necessarily have to be correct under all conditions. It is rather a reliable guide under conditions of uncertainty, a basis on which to make a decision. However, more sophisticated examples of heuristics, used by experts, normally contain indications of their scope, and the conditions under which they remain true.

3.5.5 Identifying expert heuristics

During elicitation, we must identify from what the expert says, how using heuristic guide-lines assists the expert. Since we know that this knowledge may not be explicitly or easily recalled, it would be useful to be able to spot the characteristic symptoms of heuristics when examining a transcript (Lenat, D., 1983).

In practice heuristics are easy to overlook because the elicitor is seeking clues for something implicit. In effect, the expert is looking to construct a representation of something behind the words that the expert speaks.

It is often the inability to provide an adequate reason or explanation that indicates submerged knowledge. It is very common, for instance, when asking experts how they achieve particular effects, to receive the answer: 'I can't say how, I just know'. Here is an example taken from a real transcript to illustrate the point:

> '*The trouble is, we don't really know. You must remember, the systems we have at the moment, people fly by the seat of their pants, nobody thinks they are doing anything logical at all. There are blokes out there with experience who are good at their job, er, they look at it logically obviously, but it's not really rational logic, it's sort of instinctive logic.*'

It is precisely where we meet this 'sort of instinctive logic' that the elicitor should be most alert: this is an area to be probed. Unfortunately the signals which suggest the presence of heuristics can be a lot more vague and indirect than this, therefore: take care in constructing questions; and look out continually for feedback cues which suggest the expert is struggling to express something. This might indicate a need to probe more carefully and thoroughly.

In the next chapter we will discuss the actual process of interviewing in great depth and indicate how the interview process itself can be used to help reveal the hidden ways the expert thinks.

4 Interviewing methods

4.1 INTERVIEWING IN PRACTICE

The interview is a powerful method for accessing the expert's knowledge. This chapter is committed to the practical aspects of interviewing: the organization, the costs and the techniques adapted to suit elicitation. Later, we will discuss in depth three major interviewing techniques specifically adapted to the requirements of elicitation as we have encountered them:

- the expert focused interview (Orientation)
- the structured interview
- the 'think aloud' interview

4.1.1 The nature of the interview

An interview is a formal pattern of verbal interaction. The correct interviewing techniques are essential in knowledge elicitation, since the more professional the elicitor's approach, the better the results, both in terms of the information obtained, and the ease and speed with which it is obtained. Knowledge elicitation interviews can be carried out in the short term, where a relatively simple and well understood task is to be accomplished, or long term, where a major project is undertaken. In either case many of the same considerations apply. In both cases it is essential to focus on content, effectiveness and relationships.

Even when the reader is familiar with all the complexities and pitfalls and may be aware of what to do (or what not to do), only practical application in the context of a project or an interview simulation can make good this knowledge.

There should be enough flexibility in all the techniques to adapt and modify them for different requirements. Even though the techniques are specific in method and content, structurally they can be varied to suit context, circumstances or even personal taste. The orientation interview, for instance, is supposed to be exploratory and wide ranging (wide and shallow scope), designed to give the elicitor an overview. Structurally, however, it can still be **formal** resulting in a short, straightforward sequence of questions and answers, where it is important to gain as much relevant information in the shortest amount of time, or **informal** where the interview is more loose and can range over many subjects and areas without, on the surface at least, appearing to have much direction.

Both types have their particular characteristics, and benefits, and are used to gain different types or levels of knowledge.

4.1.2 Recording information

There are several possible methods for recording the interview information: tape recording, video recording, making notes and relying purely on memory. We shall be discussing tape recording below in detail as this is the main contender for record keeping. Video recording tends to be used specifically where there are circumstances which prevent the use of, or make difficult, techniques relying on language. Of course video recording can be used to augment other recording methods, and to enhance other training and teaching materials. There are specialized difficulties involved in its use (availability, cost and experience and so on) which make it too large and too specialist a subject for detailed treatment here. During and after the interview, using some kind of shorthand or code is common but suffers from some distinct advantages, which will emerge in the discussion below. Memory is the least reliable. Practitioners who rely solely on their own memory as a reliable means of record keeping invite disaster. Despite this many do.

4.1.3 Tape recording

The basic advantage of tape recording over other methods is that no verbal material is lost (providing sound levels and voice fidelity are adequate). Comparisons of tape recordings with written interview transcripts indicate that remarkably large amounts of material are lost in the written transcripts based on notes. The loss may be as high as 75 per cent or above (Bucher, R., 1956).

Certainly the recall of interview material fades rapidly over time. Elicitors will most likely remember what they, personally, found interesting or easier to remember. It is essential, in elicitation, that all the important facts are remembered in context, but it may not be apparent at any given moment just what is significant, and what is not. A recording allows the elicitor to go back and listen to the interview in the light of new understanding, whereas a written transcript, unless it is verbatim, does not. Furthermore a tape recording preserves the inflection and emphasis of the expert's voice, which might also provide information. Thus recording can have hidden efficiency benefits.

There is no prior formula for judging whether or not tape recorded interviews are feasible, or even desirable, for a given project. It does cost more, and might not be suitable on that ground alone. The environmental conditions in which the elicitation is to take place might rule tape recording out, and so on (Belson, W., 1967).

The effect of tape recording on information

The decision to make tape recordings will be based on the nature of the project, the additional expenditure of time and money for transcription, and whether the information to be recorded is complex and very extensive; personal, in which case a participant may not want a recording, or may at least want control of any recording, or assurances on confidentiality; and sensitive, where for instance matters of official or military secrecy are involved, and the question is one of secrecy rather than just discretion.

Three problems considered

1. Will the use of a tape recorder increase the expert's resistance to the interview and thereby raise the question refusal rate?

Research has shown that resistance is encountered very rarely (Bucher). If the expert does resist tape recording, then it is either because of fear concerning what will happen to the information on the tape (and who will hear it), or fears that the information will be used for an unknown and possibly illegitimate purpose. The expert should know who will use the knowledge, who will listen to the tape recordings and for what purpose they will be used. It is also wise to offer the expert a transcript or summary of the elicitor's findings, this may also help to lower resistance to tape recording. The expert may then correct, add or alter any of these findings, which will serve several purposes:

- it ensures that the expert and elicitor understand one another, indicating any misunderstandings before they do any damage;
- it enables the expert to keep track of progress and feel that the elicitation is going somewhere;
- it calms the expert's fears of misrepresentation, and allowing to deal with any problems that arise as they appear, rather than having to deal with their consequences later.

During the initial interviews, the expert tends to be apprehensive and may feel uncomfortable with the tape recorder, but this soon disappears. Even so the elicitor should make it clear that the expert may switch off the recorder to make remarks that should not be recorded. The tape recorder is merely a tool, and should be under the mutually agreed control of both parties. It should not become an unwelcome intrusion.

2. Will the presence of the tape recorder decrease or destroy elicitor-expert rapport?

The tape recorder usually enhances rapport, since freedom from note-taking enables the elicitor to concentrate more fully on what the expert is saying, and developing an understanding of both the expertise and the expert. Recording permits the free-flowing qualities of face to face conversation, and eliminates the disrupting discontinuity so characteristic of a note-taking interviewing session. In technical domains the expert may feel more confident that difficult concepts or calculations will be recorded accurately. There may be situations due to sensitivity of information, or high costs when taping the interview may not be necessary.

3. Will the presence of the tape recorder alter the responses of the expert?

The question as to whether or not information will be affected by tape recording should be answered empirically. If it is felt that some subject matter is likely to be affected by tape recording then it might be better to mix the techniques, using tape recording or written interviews where each is appropriate. For example, the expert may wish to conceal sensitive information or withhold ideas and opinions that are, say controversial. The expert might disagree with colleagues and the methods they use.

4.1.4 The advantages of tape recording

Although there is a need to think carefully before tape recording, there are substantial advantages which should also be carefully considered. The advantages of tape-recording the interview are that it lessens distortion, bias and emphasis. The project is not prone to the many possible types of distortion often found in written interviews. Taping overcomes the natural tendency on the part of the note-taker to omit information, elaborate or condense inaccurately, and so lessen bias. Taping eliminates a major source of interviewing bias; averting the possibility of the elicitor exercising conscious or unconscious selection of what material to note down and promotes the right emphasis. Taping preserves emphasis. In a transcript based on notes, there could be a proportionate loss of emphasis on occasions where the interviewer probes or queries.

Taping permits more information to be stored, and allows later review. It provides a more objective basis for evaluating the performance of the elicitor. Another expert (or elicitor) may subsequently go back to the interview and further assess the usefulness or accuracy of information.

During an interview, the expert normally covers many areas of the work, jumping freely from one concept or fact to another, as the performance of the task dictates. In contrast the elicitor may wish to concentrate on one area, and expectations are therefore set for hearing that particular range of information. Thus the elicitor concentrates on the particular range of information required to build understanding at that point, and ignores the rest. If the interview has been recorded, and in the later stages of elicitation these other areas become important, the elicitor can backtrack through the old tape transcripts. Listening to the tape recording again reactivates memory, and preserves these areas. Where the transcript depended on notes it is more likely that secondary aspects would have been ignored in the first place and more interviews would be necessary to capture them later. The authors advocate taping the interview without taking notes as well, but the decision to do so is really down to the particular preferences and circumstances of the elicitor and expert.

• Taping facilitates review of the elicitation process. Further, participants in recorded interviews generally give more serious consideration to what they say than in unrecorded interviews.
• Reviewing — the process of an elicitation can be especially useful for training purposes. Practitioners need to understand the extent to which the results of an interview are determined by the

elicitor's interviewing technique, or lack of it. Tape recording permits a reviewer to make a more critical evaluation of the elicitor's effect on the information.

- Recreating — a 'live' interview enables the instructor to make training much more realistic and pertinent than if written methods are used. Tape recordings of the novice in action also enables the review of the major weaknesses or errors of inexperience in context, which allows the process of learning to be fine tuned to a much greater degree.
- Complexity — taping assists the elicitor to cope with complexity. Expertise often consists of a tangled and complex skein of facts, objects, concepts, and the relationships and interdependencies between them. The taped interview enables the elicitor to go repeatedly through such material until it can be understood.
- New information — the cues for information that may have been missed are retained on tape, and the elicitor can return to that part of the interview and following up on any new area of knowledge.
- Control — tape recordings are also extremely valuable for continuity and direction. Even some time after the original interview took place, the elicitor can review the tape to decide what the next interview should be about. This helps to ensure that all areas are properly covered by an appropriate developmental sequence of subsequent interviews.
- Freedom — the recorded interview has a liberating influence on the elicitor who is freed from the tedious and absorbing task of note-taking, concentrating full attention on the process, and the more subtle interactive aspects of the interview.
- Efficiency — taping enhances efficiency. The elicitor, using a tape recorder, is able to obtain more interviews during a given time period than an elicitor who takes notes, or attempts to reconstruct the interview from memory after completion. Recording eliminates the time and labour spent rewriting from notes, correcting, checking and re-editing the interview.
- Self-awareness — is enhanced. The objectivity provided by the elicitor on hearing the performance aids developing a greater sensitivity and awareness of the interviewing process and how the elicitor affects it.

It would be impossible to point out failings and omissions to a prospective elicitor during an actual interview, and it is more difficult to rectify these failings at a later date. Hearing yourself on tape is a sobering experience, but it is a very practical way of understanding how your technique sounds to the expert or anyone else.

4.1.5 The cost of transcription

By far the greatest expenditure of time and money is connected with transcribing the original tape into a verbatim transcript, or into edited hard copy. These costs are sometimes so large that the decision to transcribe must be incorporated into the project design and budget at the outset. The decision to tape the interview must be considered before the project starts because the time and cost factors are so large that in some projects where there may also be other extreme constraints, such as environmental, recording all interviews would not be possible.

It may not be necessary to transcribe if:

• the interview is highly structured;
• the length is (relatively) short;
• the information is only needed for background;
• the material is of a sensitive nature;
• the content gives general impressions rather than specific details;
• a colleague is taking notes on a particular area of enquiry.

It should be noted however that any project that requires detailed content analysis of the interviews will certainly need typewritten manuscripts of the recordings.

4.1.6 Estimating

The cost of the interview is given by the number of pages per hour of tape and per hour for checking, proof reading and correction of the typescript. The direct money cost for each hour of original recording (including the cost of the tapes) will be:

• cost of elicitor (time per person hour)
• cost of assistant (time per person hour)
• cost of audio typist (time for transcriptions per person hour)
• initial cost of tape recorder and tapes
• cost of paper, computer, discs, etc.
• costs of repair and maintenance of the recording equipment and computer or word processor
• cost of person hours for the meetings to arrange elicitation schedules, etc.

(Note that the expert's time has to be included in the overall cost of the project.)

• cost of expert (time per person hour).

We will assume the duration of the elicitation interview to be on average 2 hours. Using word processors the time taken for transcribing could be 5 hours (or possibly more) for every hour of recording. Many elicitors do their own transcribing and thus it would take them 1 or 2 hours longer overall if they are not proficient audio typists. Some time is saved because, even if the elicitor does transcribe verbatim, any obvious irrelevances can be edited out.

The following example gives an idea of the total person hours required for the iterative cycle of interviewing, transcribing, proof reading, checking, analysis and preparation for the next interview.

For example, the estimates for a feasibility study would be:

5 interviews of 2 hours each   10 interview hours   (I = 10)

For each hour of interview:

• transcription time   6 hours   (T = 6)
• proof reading   2.5 hours   (P = 2.5)
• analysis and preparation   15 hours   (A = 15)

For each hour of interview the time taken is:

• 1 hour for the interview
• 6 hours for the transcription
• 2½ hours for the proof reading
• 15 hours for the analysis and preparation

which is the same as (1 + 6 + 2.5 + 15) = 24.5 hours.

If the project involves 10 hours of interviews, then the person hours involved is 24.5 × 10 = 245 = 7 weeks.

Therefore as a general rule for a given project the total number of person hours needed can be calculated as the number 24.5 times the number of interview hours, or:

$$I * (I + T + P + A)$$

where: I is the number of interview hours, T is the transcription time for each interview hour, P is the proof reading time for each interview hour and A is the analysis and preparation time for each interview hour. In this case I = 10; T = 6; P = 2.5; A = 15.

An example of an actual large study shows that:

30 tape recorded interviews, based on the above figures for transcription, specifically, for each hour of original recording, an additional 6.3 hours of skilled typing time, and 2.8 hours of checking time were required:

$$30 * (1 + 6.3 + 2.8 + 15)$$
$$= 30 * 25.1$$
$$= 753 \ hours$$

assuming the following approximations: an average effort of 5 hours per day (a generous allowance in practice), a full 5 day week, and 4.5 working weeks in a month:

753 hours = 150 days = 30 weeks = 6 months (approximately)

and

*Total transcription time = 30 * 6.3   = 189 hours*

*Total proof reading time = 30 * 2.8   = 84 hours*
*Total analysis and preparation time = 30 * 15   = 450 hours*

This should illustrate how costly the tape recording could be in a large study, and how important it is to consider the ramifications of transcription, which are all to often not considered.

Remember also that transcription and checking time will vary somewhat in relation to:

• the intelligibility of the original recording;
• the elicitor's or typist's speed;
• the degree of familiarity with the dialect or accent of the expert and elicitor;
• unfamiliar technical terminology;
• talking speed;
• interview and dialogue structure;
• environmental or task cues (i.e. if a device or form was used as focus).

The 5 to 1 transcription ratio and the 1 to 1 checking ratio would appear to be a realistic average upon which to base time and budgeting estimates.

• The checking time in the elicitation transcripts do not allow for accurate spelling or punctuation, but checks are essential to ensure the factual and scientific accuracy. These will sometimes have to be re-checked with the expert.
• A audio typist's machine is an efficient way of listening to the tapes for transcription purposes as the tape can be stopped by the operator to deal with the material in convenient chunks.

• When the elicitor puts a tape back into its cover, the same identification information can be on the tape label as was recorded initially on the tape at the beginning of the interview. It enables the elicitor and others to find a particular tape from the rest immediately, and classifies the knowledge each tape holds. This simple procedure, surprisingly, is often not done.

4.1.7 Two golden rules for tape recording interviews

Rule 1) Write clear notes on the content of each interview to accompany the tape. At the beginning of each tape, either before or during the interview, state what date it is, the time, who is participating and the proposed subject or area to be elicited.

This method of labelling the interview with numbers, participants and subject matter, etc. is essential: if the markings on either the tape or tape cover are lost, or if the tape has been put into the wrong case, the content is still identifiable. This procedure should be applied to all interview tape recordings.

Rule 2) Time should be allowed for completion of the analysis before the next stage of elicitation begins.

In practice this is sometimes impossible to achieve, because of factors such as: accessibility of the expert, environmental conditions, difficulty or lack of audio-typing facilities, severe time restraints, departmental or management directives.

It is more sensible to halt interviewing and finish analysis than to try and cope with an increasing amount of information which is impossible to analyse in the time given. Late transcribing may also lead to delay and complicates the process of analysis. Any time lag between completing these stages may play havoc with deadlines unless some careful planning has been done. If nothing can be done, then inform those concerned with the project that further elicitation without analysis will be detrimental to the project. It is essential to make this point explicit, or the elicitor may find that there is continual pressure on all other projects to work under the same unfavourable conditions.

4.1.8 Scheduling the interview cycle

We recommend that the elicitation process take the form of an iterative cycle:

1. Interview
2. Transcription
3. Proof reading
4. Analysis and preparation (for the next interview)

In this way the elicitor can follow through smoothly from one interview through to analysis and preparation of the next interview without interruption. Concentration can be maintained on a particular area and a more thorough analysis of it made.

In knowledge elicitation it is more appropriate to think in terms of elapsed time rather than person hours. This must be taken into account in judging the total number of weeks the project will take. Where the elicitor uses audio-typists to transcribe interviews, it is best to avoid being idle while waiting for the results. Using an approximate example, if there are two typists transcribing, then out of five days only the second day is 'vacant', that is:

Day 1 preparation and interviewing,
Day 2 transcribing,
Day 3 proof reading,
Day 4 and 5 analysis and preparation.

The analysis phase should be started as soon after the interview as possible, so that memory of the content of the interview is optimal. If the elicitor has an assistant and time is short, then another alternative is to stagger the interviews as shown below:

1st Interview = (a) and 2nd Interview = (b)
Day 1 Interview (a),
Day 2 Interview transcription (a) and interview (b),
Day 3 Proof reading of interview (a) and transcription (b),
Day 4 Analysis and preparation (a) and proof reading (b),
Day 5 Analysis and preparation (b).

The drawback with this method is the extra workload imposed by the transcript analysis. The elicitor must give one interview and, when it is finished, review the previous interview's contents, this can be jarring since the elicitor's mental set is for the most recent material. Also the lack of continuity makes it more of an effort to locate the information pertinent to particular points of analysis. If there is sufficient continuity in the subject matter however, this may not present insurmountable difficulties. Marking the tape with time date and subject matter will ease this dislocation of subject matter (this should be done on all tapes whatever the method used).

The elicitor will have a hopeless task ahead if attempts to perform all the analysis are made at the same time. The elicitor controls the rate of information acquired and thus ensures that each part can be completed in the time required, using:

- The orientation interview for general information.
- The more structured, detailed interview for more detailed knowledge.
- The expert's examples of how a task(s) is performed for strategic knowledge.
- A short review for checking the results so far at the beginning of every new interview.

The different types of interview described briefly above are discussed fully in Section 4.4.

4.2 PREPARATION FOR INTERVIEWING

People who do not think about the manner in which they ask questions usually do not care about the answers they receive. In knowledge elicitation the questions and the answers are the foundations and the building blocks of knowledge itself, and great care should be taken in their design.

4.2.1 Preparatory discussion

The expert and the elicitor should meet before elicitation begins to discuss certain important factors:

- The purpose and the nature of the elicitation interviews.
- What factors are going to influence the progress of the interviews?
- Are there any special arrangements to be made? Special equipment?
- Is it clear from the outset roughly in which direction the whole project is going, or is there a need to make alternative or contingency plans?
- The environmental setting of the interview.

It is important to find out if the expert would prefer a quiet room rather than a noisy work environment, or another more neutral location for the first few orientation interviews.

It is important that the expert's normal environment is used in later elicitation interviews, otherwise realistic behavioural cues may be missed.

- Can the expert only be interviewed while doing a task?
- The timing of the interviews must be agreed upon.
- How many hours is the expert available for elicitation, and how many hours per session?
- How long would the expert consider convenient, necessary, or too tiring? (this can be altered accordingly).
- Are there to be any 'breaks' within a session, when should they be taken and for how long?
- If the interview goes on for longer than an hour it is advisable to plan a break, even if only a short one.

It is important to maintain a high level of mental sharpness for all the participants and in this respect breaking is not time wasting nor a luxury.

How many interviews is it possible to hold in one week, bearing in mind the arrangements to be made for the interviews to be transcribed? Will the elicitor have enough time in which to listen, read, analyse and prepare for the next interview? (dependent on the interview material and the ease in which it can be analysed).

The elicitor should come to the first meeting with some examples of interview schedules. The schedule should be agreed with the expert so the understanding is that any alteration to the schedule has an effect on all the other processes (transcription, analysis, preparation, etc). The elicitor should explain the need for the schedule, so that if the expert cancels an interview, or the amount of interviewing time agreed rises, then the schedule will have to be altered accordingly.

The elicitor and expert must be prepared for a schedule that may require frequent updating. Will the expert agree to being tape recorded? If the expert does not, what alternatives, such as note-taking, can be agreed?

4.2.2 Equipment

If the expert agrees to participate then the elicitor must have all the right equipment: a good stereo tape recorder with a reverse mechanism, fresh batteries or re-chargeable (and re-charged) ones, tapes, good quality microphone(s), a small back up tape recorder (just in case something goes wrong with the main recorder). These machines and their accompanying equipment should be tested beforehand and the elicitor should ensure he or she is proficient in their use. Trying to eliminate whistling noises from the microphone just as the interview is about to start does not create a very good impression. Information lost on a tape, or a malfunctioning tape recorder, could be the equivalent of 4 person-hours work (the elicitor and expert in a 2 hour long elicitation interview). Error may creep in if the tape is mis-heard or a statement is mis-interpreted as something seemingly plausible but actually wrong.

If there is any doubt it is better to verify that material again with the expert. This can be time consuming, so it is better to take pains to get it right the first time. Careless mistakes can cause considerable, avoidable waste. The entire interview might have to be repeated, the subject area will have lost its freshness, and the participant's enthusiasm may begin to wane. Worse still, some of the information itself may be lost in subsequent interviews because of confusion about what has, or has not, previously been said.

Alternatives

If recording is not possible, the elicitor could use an assistant to record information during the interview. The elicitor is then free to explore with the expert with less loss of information. However it is important to determine why the expert does not want recording to take place if this is the case. The expert's reluctance may stem from a lack of knowledge about the elicitation process, and the importance of getting an accurate record. It may be that the expert just feels apprehensive and can be persuaded to overcome these feelings for the sake of increased accuracy and efficiency.

Practical arrangements should be checked. For example, does the room or setting have an electric plug near the seating area? If not the elicitor must bring fresh tape recorder batteries with him. Seemingly unimportant details such as this can cause endless difficulties and wasted time if overlooked.

All aspects subsequent to the actual interview should be checked. The typists, or whoever will transcribe the tape-recorded interview, must be informed before the elicitation interviews how much work and time will be involved in transcribing the tapes, so that the finished product will meet the agreed deadlines. Everyone involved must also be aware that schedules may change and should be able to adapt to that eventuality.

Ensure that all transcripts are clearly identified. We believe this to be worth repeating: before the start of every interview it is essential to record the name of elicitor, the expert, the date and subject of the interview, where the interview is taking place and any other relevant information.

4.2.3 Maintaining awareness during the interview

Because of the importance of these issues, we will briefly recapitulate some points discussed elsewhere but crucial for the elicitor to bear in mind these points. Remember always to be critical of any information received. It is so easy to be lulled into a false sense of security by the authority of the expert. Reporting may be generally accurate, but may, nevertheless, leave out a great deal of relevant and important information. The expert will not know what information is omitted; there will only be an indication. The expert will sometimes say something that is not the case in practice.
The expert may not:

- give the exact goal-seeking behaviour or all the problem-solving sequences,
- the full range of concepts, or all the information needed,
- state exactly how the expert does the task on every occasion every time it is done
- gives answers at the right level of detail and so on, depending on the context.

It would be impertinent to argue or contradict the expert outright, but it is quite reasonable to plan checks and verification. Most experts are willing to cooperate and assist this process.

Case history

An example of a case history describes some of the difficulties that can occur in verification. An elicitor wished to learn how a fingerprint expert identified two fingerprints as belonging to the same person. One fingerprint was 'perfect', and the other was taken from the scene of a crime, and therefore imperfect, as some parts of the print were smudged or missing. He talked to the expert, and then conducted as experiment in which he tested the information the expert had given him. The expert said he identifies similarities in fingerprints, first by rotating the prints around a common axis to see if there was any degree of match. He then tests the hypothesis that one fingerprint is the same as the other by looking for similarities of contour 'events', such as endings, whorls, etc. and tries to match these with events on the other print.

The expert did not consider the contour 'grooves' on the prints however. He did not believe these grooves were important orientation clues for him. So the elicitor put this to the test by removing this aspect during an attempt by the expert to make a match. As a result, the expert could no longer match the fingerprints, and requested the grooves to be reinstated, proving that the expert did use the grooves to provide some orientation, even though he was unaware of the fact (Personal communication. Ebi Adhami, 1986). This example points to the importance of some kind of experimental testing of behaviour, especially if the dependent information is visual or motor.

Note also that as the expert gains familiarity with the elicitation process, he/she will begin to relax and understand the need to be more thoughtful and thorough when reporting. The selected interviewing techniques described in Section 4.4 will aid the expert to think more deeply and methodically about the expertise.

4.3 INTERVIEW ORIENTATION

During the orientation stage the elicitor first gets to grips with the overall nature of the expert's knowledge, unless the project involved a feasibility study which counts as orientation. It is useful to start with a high level view of:

- the scope of the domain,
- the expert's task in outline, the main topics, concepts, and procedures of the performance,
- the views which the elicitor will use to control the quantity of information,
- a few simple representative examples of problem types and how the expert would go about solving them.

The elicitor requires some familiarity with terminology, and some insights into the personality of the expert and the characteristic ways of expression.

4.3.1 Orientation interviews

These interviews should be like normal, interesting and informative conversations. They should be relaxed and unhurried in character. The elicitor should acquire whatever general information is needed over several interviews, depending on the size and complexity of the domain. The elicitor should listen attentively to the expert, and try to help the expert to relax and be at ease with the process of elicitation.

The first interviews should be analysed for the setting, timing, the expert's personality, the elicitor's own performance, and the overall impressions during the interview.

Vital information for future interactions can be assessed and fed back into the process right from the start. Early impressions should be noted and subjected to scrutiny. When more familiarity is acquired as the process proceeds it will be harder and harder to identify these early impressions. Not that initial impressions are necessarily more correct than later ones, but the initial stages provide a unique opportunity to use intuitions which are most active during initial encounters. Like any other source of information they must be treated critically, however.

4.3.2 Questions to ask arising from the interview

- Were there any problems, and, if there were, of what nature?, how and why did they occur, and how, if at all, could they be resolved?
- How well did the expert participate? Was the expert happy to participate?
- Was the interview too long? Did the expert become tired?
- Was the setting, seating, noise level right? Could they be improved upon?
- Were there interruptions (phones ringing, colleagues entering, etc) what could be done about them, were the coffee breaks welcome or intrusive, etc?
- What did the elicitor find difficult, or easy, and how could it be changed or adapted to make the elicitation process easier, or quicker?

Thinking about how the participants reacted to each other, the conditions of the environment, how the participants were affected by the environment, could eradicate, or at least ease, some of the difficulties encountered, and should make further interviewing that much easier.

4.4 THE INTERVIEWING TECHNIQUES

The following paragraphs describe the various methods of interviewing. These interviewing techniques impose an artificial structure on recall of the expert's knowledge, like building a scaffold when erecting a building. In order to understand the actual structure or arrangement of the expert's knowledge, we must first provide a framework so that we can take some deliberate steps towards understanding. It is undoubtedly frustrating for the expert to remember the knowledge in this way, but this is easily compensated for by the ease with which such high level information can be processed and used for implementation.

Without understanding the background to the interviewing techniques, experts will naturally be inclined to talk about their knowledge in a linear fashion, following a problem through from start to finish, bringing in knowledge from many different sources, sometimes including aspects seemingly unconnected. It will require some effort on the part of the expert to disconnect aspects of their knowledge which fit naturally together, so explaining what the procedures are intended to achieve should help when asking the expert to make the effort. It will seem much more reasonable if the expert knows why it is needed and he/she will usually put up with this inconvenience more readily.

4.4.1 The orientation interview

In these initial interviews the elicitor allows the expert to speak more freely about the expertise, within the mutually agreed limits of scope and Domain View. The elicitor will already have explained what type of information is wanted at this stage, e.g. either a global view of the domain, or particular view under discussion, and the expert's function and task within it. The elicitor only intervenes to direct the expert with general questions and listens while the expert outlines an area in high level terms.

The elicitor and expert should both understand the type and level of information required, that is, for the orientation interview, not detailed information but basic concepts, problems and tasks. Detailed information will be required later on, in the second stage of elicitation, at present, general information about each of the views will be sufficient.

More specifically, this technique is used to elicit general knowledge (surface knowledge) about a subject area. The interviewer will use the result of these interviews to extract more information in later sessions using more penetrating questions to probe deeper, these also being derived from developing an understanding of the domain. The elicitor acts as an interpreter. The elicitor stands between the expert's behaviour in the performance of a task, and some explicit representation of that behaviour, which will be uncovered.

The orientation technique ensures control of the volume of new knowledge. Should the expert begin to stray onto other areas, or begin to go into too much detail, the elicitor must be prepared to step in politely and redirect the proceedings, guiding the expert back to the information that is required at this stage. This is a statement of the ideal case; in practice it is exceedingly difficult to know just what is and isn't relevant, but that very lack of understanding triggers the elicitor to respond when feeling overwhelmed by detail.

Try to maintain the correct level of detail. The degree of strictness about concentrating on a particular view, given that the expert will tend to move freely over the whole area of understanding, will depend on how much, and how well, the elicitor's understanding of the expertise is growing.

As a rule of thumb the elicitor does not intervene or interrupt the flow unless there is a specific problem, but obviously if the elicitor gets too confused there must be some intervention. The elicitor must use judgement based on experience, gained either through real interviews or simulations.

Using the technique

The elicitor introduces the main view areas to the expert and should begin by asking general orientation questions:

- 'Could you describe, in simple terms, what you do?'
- 'What do you consider to be your main task?'
- 'What is your main problem?'

As far as possible, allow the expert to talk without interruption. If the elicitor does not interrupt too much, it allows the expert's ideas to flow more easily, also allowing them to become generally more relaxed, free to talk about what they do, and spontaneously offer views on how it is done. Asking too many questions will distort the interview towards the elicitor's preconceptions and reactions rather than deliver what the expert actually knows.

Do not ask another question until the expert has completely come to the end of the explanation. It is common for elicitors to ask a question as soon as the expert ceases to speak. A small pause will often encourage the expert to add some more information or qualify what has already been said. Small silences may indicate that the expert wishes briefly to think about a subject; it is distracting to be directed away immediately to something else.

Encourage the expert to speak freely. If the expert is encouraged to speak freely from the outset, and allowed to volunteer infor- mation spontaneously, later explanations, about more complex tasks, and descriptions of the more intricate domain characteristics, will be more clear because the expert has had some practice at explaining (if it is needed) and is used to talking during interview conditions. If the elicitor does need to interrupt, it must be done politely and diplomatically, waiting if necessary for an opportune moment to turn the expert's attention back to some problem, or away to another subject. The elicitor should encourage the expert when speaking by showing interest visually, i.e., eye contact and nodding etc. Imagine the expert was appraising your performance; it should not be all a one way flow of information or authority.

Use a checklist of aspects to be covered in an interview. It is wise to have some form of checklist, of questions, views, problems (or whatever is relevant), especially for the novice, but useful even for experienced practitioners too. The elicitor can then check off these items of information as the interview progresses ensuring that everything is covered. Later on, the list can be used as a quick reminder of what was done during a particular session, or as a prompt, indicating where roughly to look for a particular category of information.

The function of memory in orientation interviewing

The orientation interview should present no difficulty for the expert who should be able to call on generalizations and ideas that reside mostly in long-term memory, and are therefore easy to recall.

If the expert is prone to jump down a level and describe detailed information, the elicitor must redirect the area. The expert may not remember to respect the view divisions, falling back into the old, more familiar way of jumping about, both in terms of complexity and focus. It is then difficult for the elicitor to assess this information because it is too early for real familiarity, at this stage, with the way the expert thinks. This 'level jumping' may in some situations provide interesting insights or examples, but if the expert continually jumps levels then the elicitor may quickly lose direction. The elicitor must re-establish that direction and level with the expert or lose control of the interview itself.

Problems that may occur

Problems occur in interviewing when the elicitor is either not prepared for an occurrence, or does not know how to behave under specific circumstances. The opportunities for problems, if not infinite, are numerous. It will depend on such diverse factors as:

- how much experience the expert/elicitor has;
- the attitude and cooperativeness of the expert;
- how much, and what kinds of, external and 'political' pressures are affecting progress;
- the size and degree of complexity of the expertise;
- difficulties with the environment;
- constraints on the expert's performance;
- problems translating the expertise into an objective representation.

It would be impossible to be comprehensive and anticipate every possible difficulty. Some key situations we have encountered are discussed below, and suggestions are made to remedy them.

1. The expert has difficulty recalling information, or can't get started easily.

It may be helpful to start with another view of the domain instead, one that the expert isn't blocking on, and that would interest the expert and elicitor more.

2. The expert is nervous, or not familiar with the interview situation, or for some other reason may want some guidance from the elicitor.

The elicitor must ensure at the beginning of these sessions, politely repeating it as often as necessary, that it is the expert who should describe, explain and illustrate, while the elicitor listens and occasionally probes. All new procedures seem awkward at first but this wears off. Some patience and a little gentle insistence usually does the trick.

3. The elicitor is too wordy in the initial interviews.

The elicitor must strike the right balance. If too dominant or too verbose, the expert will sense that some self-importance is being diminished, and react passively instead of coming forward with the necessary information. It is useless to outline respective roles if the elicitor then contradicts them in practice, especially if the expert follows the elicitor's lead, responding passively instead of taking the active, initiating role required.

The elicitor then may lose some control of the interview because of this conflict. Control does not indicate a constant flow of questions. It is sensible to have one question in reserve but it is not necessary to 'drive' the content of the interview by constant questioning. An elicitor who plays ego games is doomed, as is any project on which the elicitor works. Similarly, the elicitor will receive less information from an expert who is more interested in establishing self-image, or is trying to find a 'place' in the interview situation. It is essential that the elicitor fulfils a role of helping the expert adjust and to understand the tasks they both have to perform.

4. The expert displays symptoms which suggest tension.

- Does the expert talk down to the elicitor?
- Is the expert a trifle pompous about self-skills?
- Does the expert try to blind the elicitor with expertise?
- Is there a reluctance to give much information? Is jargon used to confuse, and so receive some satisfaction from the elicitor's ignorance?

All these behaviour patterns indicate that the expert is feeling insecure or has some objection to being interviewed, even perhaps that the elicitor too is posing some threat to the interviewee's professional competence. Some of this may be true, at least in part. The expert may feel that knowledge is being exploited, and want to retain some of it, to keep a position of power. If this sort of behaviour is making elicitation difficult, it may be necessary to halt the process and get to the root of the problem before real progress can be made.

- Is the expert irritable when asked certain questions?
The expert may be less informative about some issues in order to maintain a certain opinion. Analyse this rejection of questions. On the other hand, it may be because what the elicitor is asking is out of context, irrelevant, unimportant, repetitive, or outside the domain of the expert. Ask the expert directly about the problem if necessary.

- Does the expert sidestep the elicitor's requests?
How experts convey their knowledge at work will colour how they convey their knowledge to the elicitor. Excessively diplomatic answers can mean the expert has difficulty in conveying information normally considered unwelcome to the recipient. For example, one expert had the habit of answering all the elicitor's questions initially with 'Yes', and then proceeded with some skill to explain why the elicitor's view was not correct. This was because the expert frequently had to give information that was often distressing for the recipient. If the expert constantly conveys information to sub-ordinates or superiors then this sort of behaviour may be reflected in the way the expert answers questions, that is, patronizingly or diplomatically, in detail or superficially. The elicitor has to be wary

that simplistic or superficial answers do not obscure the real views of the expert.

The expert may be in the habit of using certain terminology to clients to promote understanding of the problem and not confuse them with unnecessary technical details. Generally, the point remains that if the elicitor fails to understand, then the project fails. It is really a question of how motivated the elicitor and the expert are to succeed. Obstruction, whether or not it is intended, inhibits success, and can only be overcome by understanding the expert's motivation, or halting any power struggle that may exist by understanding them. If these problems are not solved, they will continually threaten the results of the elicitation.

5. The expert implies things without saying them directly, or is inclined not to follow a thought or sentence through.

It is very easy to assume, especially when deeply involved with something for a long time, that 'everybody knows that', or that because the elicitor has established a superficial knowledge, the expert thinks the elicitor knows more than is really the case. The elicitor must be constantly on the lookout for this, and be prepared to speak up when something is not clear. It is vital, and not always easy, to be honest and confess ignorance, apparently at the cost of losing some face, but the damage of not doing so is likely to spread throughout the project and threaten its success.

If the expert tails off at the end of sentences, perhaps lack of confidence is the cause, or perhaps the expert is just concentrating on the next thought. It is important to find out, otherwise much time may be wasted and essential information lost, if the problem is ignored.

6. The expert uses too many words and sentences to describe a simple concept.

Concentrate on the content and less on the way the expert describes it. Information that seems to be simple may have a component of difficulty that the elicitor is not aware of.

The expert may not be able to explain things simply or there may be an assumption that the elicitor has understood the knowledge. If the elicitor cannot discern the reason, the next best thing is to ask the expert if there is a complicating factor in the information that is given. If this phenomenon persists and the elicitor is using unnecessary tape time, precis what the expert has said and read it back: 'I'm rather confused, but what I have understood you to have said is this, etc', and relate in short precise form, i.e. 'this' is really what I want.

The expert may continue with discursive comments, not realizing what is required. Sometimes it is possible to confine length by shortening the interview and meeting more often in the week. If the interview is shorter, it quickens the pace and hopefully the pace of the output. A more structured interview may be necessary, as a last resort, but beware of resulting misconceptions and omission of essential information. Explain that specific information is not needed at this stage, but stress that, later on, this information will be invaluable.

The application of any technique must be measured against its suitability. If the elicitor felt in advance that this (or any other) approach was unlikely to yield good results then it is the elicitor's responsibility to seek something better. In fact it may be necessary to be experimental. The ideas suggested throughout this book were modifications of original but untried ideas, only by application and experiment did they grow into their present form, but they remain generalized suggestions: the practitioner must always be ready to adapt, modify or try something new.

7. The expert is prone to instruct and lecture, and does not like to be interrupted, even politely.

The expert may have taken the old adage 'knowledge is power' too seriously. Being an authority on any subject does not necessarily entitle someone to act as though they have power over others. The implicit danger lying behind instruction is that the expert might omit material, or not explain it in detail because the expert feels it is far beyond the elicitor's understanding. The expert should be encouraged to treat the elicitor as an equal. There is, of course, an element of teaching involved in transferring knowledge from one person to another, and some instruction is more likely, and acceptable, early on in the process. If this pattern is allowed to continue into the later stages however it will become increasingly difficult to change. To avoid this, the elicitor might try using more structured and directional interviewing techniques in subsequent interviews.

This behaviour may be a cover for fears the expert has about the subject. The expert may fear not seeming to be authoritative, or scientific enough, or acceptable to other experts, and so on. Assuming the role of teacher may be a habit, but puts smooth knowledge transfer at risk, therefore this behaviour should be diplomatically discouraged. Any knowledge that is acquired should be cross-checked against actual performance during a realistic task or problem situation.

8. The expert may place more emphasis on theory and method, but less on practice.

Where there is a body of theory connected to a domain, it will possibly make the task of verification easier. Although it is commonly the case that the expert is required just at the point where theory is inadequate and heuristics based on experience and long practice are the best guide. However, sometimes an expert may have a very well developed theoretical understanding without a great deal of practical experience: an academic, for example, or a military strategist who has never experienced real battle conditions.

The academic draws on, interprets and condenses the experience of others to develop an overview of the domain. Under one set of circumstances the knowledge might be invaluable: in a teaching system for instance. In another more practical context, the knowledge may be less useful because lacking essential real world components only realized in an experienced practitioner from the part of the domain to be captured.

The case of the military strategist is different again. It may be that there have simply been no opportunities for acquiring real world experience of battle. The strategist is therefore forced to base practice on simulations, war games and post-hoc analysis of previous events. Further, in this case there really is no 'science' (in the sense of the physical science paradigm) on which to base practice, but merely the 'current' strategy.

The elicitor should carefully assess the circumstances before criticizing the expert for being too theoretical. If the criticism is just, however, and the elicitor believes that the expert is stating what should happen rather than what actually does, then some pressure should be applied to get at the real practices of the expert, no matter how unsound they may seem when set against the neatness of theory. The elicitor should point out that although the expert's practice may not be well understood, it is only by investigating the reality of it that it may ultimately be incorporated into a later theoretical model. It is even possible that the process of elicitation could contribute towards this (Wellbank, M., 1983).

If it turns out that the expert actually does not possess any knowledge other than the theory, and in practice that experience is required, then the elicitor must seek another expert to fill those gaps, hopefully in cooperation with the original expert. Pure theory may not take into account the variances of the environment, human factors such as inadequacies, variations, constraints, and so on. Deviations from theory often provide the heuristics of practice. Without this information, the elicitor will never know whether the original expert is likely to miss out vital information, underestimate difficulties, and over-value certain areas of expertise.

Reviewing the orientation interview

- The information from each interview should be summarized from the transcribed documents.
- This summary, be it notes, flow charts or some other form, should be shown to the expert before the start of the next interview.

Until the elicitor's analysis of the transcript has been verified by the expert, there are a range of risks, from simple slips and inaccuracies, through to grave distortions and misunderstandings. The expert can very simply correct and clarify these issues if 5–10 minutes' review time is allowed at the start of subsequent sessions. It also has the advantage of:

- a brief résumé, recapitulating the last session;
- a reminder of where the elicitation process is going;
- what progress has already been made.

There should be a consensus between the participants on the progress of the elicitation process, continuous review of each other's roles, difficulties and assumptions.

Depending on the scope and difficulties of the domain, the elicitor can gain a high level understanding of the domain, or at least most of the views into which it has been divided, in five or six interviews. There should be enough information to understand the expert's task and any constraints under which the expert must work which will affect an eventual system. The knowledge from the orientation interview constitutes the foundation on which a detailed understanding of the expertise can be built.

4.4.2 The structured interview

The structured interview in knowledge elicitation is used primarily as the second phase of interviewing to acquire more depth, and fill out levels of detail about the expertise, uncovering its depth and complexity. Ideally, at each level the elicitor allows the expert to follow the problem through while restraining the expert from digressing from the main focus of interest.

The structured interview in practice

The elicitor directs and guides the expert towards the level of detailed information that is wanted. The elicitor prompts and questions, informs the expert of areas of doubt, and asks for explanations or clarifications. It is essential that the structured interview is prepared thoroughly in advance. The elicitor must plan the questions, prepare the expert for the areas in which clarifications and greater detail is wanted. The elicitor should always allow the expert to answer the questions fully. Even though the elicitor is now taking more control and directing the process, there is still the wish that the transcription represents the expert's contributions. If the elicitor is rationing replies, the expert will become frustrated at not being given the chance to answer properly. Allow the expert space to think and be patient for the answer. Undue prompting invites ill-considered and possibly inaccurate replies. Impatience may make the expert feel less inclined to volunteer other useful information.

If the expert brings up new information that falls into a previously undiscovered category double check that this really is something new in kind, and be prepared to organize a special short investigative session to analyse the consequences of this new material. Either make a note of the area, and continue (so long as it does not directly alter the direction or progress of the interviews already scheduled), or add the new area into a new mini-cycle of interviews.

If the new information does materially alter the pattern of knowledge so far extracted, or even looks as though it could, either re-schedule the remainder of the interviews, or deal with this part first, before going back to the old schedule.

Remember to listen for the verbal cues for qualification, or conditional information ('But', 'if' and 'when'), as these can very often be the first sign-posts to hidden or missing areas of knowledge. For example:

> Yes I do move this knob here, but, sometimes if 'this' happens, then you have to check that 'this' is done before you turn the knob.

The statement 'when this happens' might be the only indicator to a vast area of vital conditional information, or just one simple exceptional case. This is where the elicitor's ingenuity and skill at probing comes into its own.

Using the domain views

The structured interview should only be carried out in the context of one of the Domain Views. Otherwise the expert will wander over too wide an area and the depth of the information will begin to vary enormously. This may not only confuse the elicitor, but could muddle the expert, especially because the expert believes that the elicitor is supposed to direct, limit and control the information category and direction.

Using the views to gain knowledge from one category at a time may seem too artificial and inflexible. What if the expert objects? In this type of interview the elicitor needs to direct or lead the expert, but not force them.

If the expert is not sure why the elicitor prevents any wandering into other areas, and might wrongly assume, for instance, that the elicitor is just not interested, then the expert would have reason to be concerned. Hence the elicitor should:

- always signal a change of interviewing technique beforehand to the expert;
- be sure to explain the technique and what it is supposed to achieve, and be sure to check that your explanation was clear and understood;
- if possible, indicate to the expert what areas, and roughly what order these areas will be dealt with.

This not only ensures that your intentions are clear, but allows the expert to comment and make suggestions or modifications to what is proposed, allowing some control and ensuring that good ideas springing from experience of the field are not missed.

None of these things need take up much time, but not doing them can cost a lot, in confusion, misunderstanding and possible bad feeling. If the process is understood, the expert is more likely to assist the elicitor.

Factors affecting the structured interview

When the amount of information to be found and analysed increases rapidly the expert, to ensure proper control is maintained, requires flexibility in thinking and approach. In a very large domain where the information is of average complexity, making several passes through the knowledge will probably be the best method of maintaining control. At each pass the level of detail can be increased, allowing the elicitor to assimilate information more smoothly. Where the information is complex, even if not overly large in volume, the elicitor should consider further subdivision of the domain views. Where, for instance, there are a great many clusters of intricate inter-relationships, sub-division into smaller views is a better strategy, especially if they cohere naturally in a modular fashion. Clearly the elicitor must use judgement here.

The challenge for the elicitor then is to formulate succinct questions which will bring out the required information from the expert at the agreed level of detail, for later analysis and understanding. Even though greater detail is required, too much and the elicitor may lose track, spend interview time inefficiently going back over material, and opening up the possibility of duplicating effort. Too little information, and the elicitor is wasting time covering that which has already been obtained during the first (orientation) phase of the elicitation. This skill in questioning is developed through practice. The beginner can profit from simulations with an experienced practitioner. Where no real experience is available, it is possible to set up exercises based on well-known areas, taken, perhaps, from the domain in which the novice elicitor will be working. The exercise, in cooperation with a partner who will act as the expert, consists of devising increasingly complex information targets which must be achieved within a pre-set number of questions. Although artificial, this kind of exercise quickly gives the participants a feeling for what is required:

- 'Could you explain this concept to me in greater detail?';
- 'What happens here?';
- I don't understand why you do this';
- 'Why, do you get that problem?';

and so on.

The function of memory in structural interviewing

Before the interview even takes place the elicitor should give the expert the right set for the process, which will assist in bringing out appropriate information and examples [Chapter 2]. Context is often catalytic for long-term memory recall, so if the interview is not in the expert's normal environment, analyse the repercussions and compensate for the normal environment with appropriate 'stage props' as far as possible.

Problems with the structured interview

- Unexplained, incomplete and missing information will always be a problem.

In the structured interview, unlike the focused interview, the focus of attention is directed more by the elicitor who decides on what information is needed to complete the model. The elicitor must confront the gaps and discontinuities in the knowledge or risk becoming confused.

• The elicitor should try to keep an open mind and must not be myopic.

There is a natural tendency to filter out anything that does not appear relevant according to our current understanding, but since the elicitor does not have a complete understanding, there must be a conscious attempt to avoid controlling the limits of the knowledge by only acknowledging what is heard or what is thought might be heard. This means always being alert and, in turn, underlines the importance of taking breaks and using shorter sessions.

Reviewing the structured interview

It is likely that the expert may wish to qualify some of the information that was given previously, but this should not involve changes that qualitatively change the knowledge gained so far. If this did happen the whole process may have gone wrong and should be immediately reviewed. If new knowledge emerges, it should be noted and examined more fully later, so that the interview originally scheduled can proceed.

The elicitor may ask questions such as:

• 'Have I got this sequence right?'
• 'Do you do this here?'
• 'Does this flow chart show the order of your decisions correctly?'
• 'Have I included all the tasks you do on this chart?'
• 'Are all the concepts relating to this here?'

and the type of answer expected would be:

• 'Yes' or 'no, I don't. I do this here'.
• 'This one is more likely to depend on this one'.
• 'You have left this one out'.

4.4.3 The 'think aloud' interview

A 'think aloud' interview is, as the name suggests, an interview in which the expert talks while thinking. An expert is given a task similar to the one usually dealt with. The expert is asked to verbalize any thoughts on a given task. This technique is probably the closest the elicitor and expert can come to an actual working situation. It is often difficult for the expert to perform the technique at first, the more the expert is required to think the more likely there is an inclination to be silent. With gentle prompting from the elicitor, and some perseverence by the expert, the thinking aloud technique becomes easier and the expert will soon be proficient.

The Think Aloud interview comes later in the process of elicitation, and constitutes a third phase. This interview should: reveal the expert's problem solving strategies; validate the conceptual information gathered from previous sessions; reveal sequences of events; and reveal the accompanying knowledge that particular task requires. The 'Think Aloud' technique can also provide a means to check and verify the knowledge gained so far. After the expert has gained some ease with a few simplified examples, and is more comfortable with the process of thinking and reporting simultaneously, the expert can move on to real task simulations if this is possible.

The elicitor should not attempt this interview unless there is evidence that there is a good understanding of the static (the 'what') knowledge. By this stage the elicitor should have gained a good understanding of the main facts and concepts and the way they fit together. When the expert is reporting on a process the elicitor should not have to stop every few sentences to clarify the meaning of some aspect. The technique is difficult enough for the expert without being sidetracked by interruptions. The elicitor does not really understand how the expert solves a task unless there is knowledge about the use of concepts, and the nature of the task.

Example of 'think aloud' technique

The following extract from an interview transcript shows how the expert describes knowledge without interruption from the elicitor. It also shows the kind of transcript that results from this technique. The particular transcript below was set out in this style. Style does vary from one transcriber to another. The elicitor will become accustomed to different layouts and be able to analyse them without largely re-editing them first. Written verbal speech can sometimes seem confusing at first but the elicitor will soon become accustomed to it. Layout is not as important as content, and the elicitor will soon be able to disregard idiosyncratic elements with practice.

Note that it is essential to possess a prior understanding of the concepts, abbreviations and terminology that the expert uses. In this example the expert was aware of the terms not used before and incorporated explanations when it was thought necessary. The vocal noise, ('umms' and 'urrs') were omitted from the transcripts as were any irrelevant asides, although the verbal 'style' of the expert remains.

'Yes, it just copies the data set from one place to another and then kicks off BDTs which then do the processing, creates new datasets and if the Infograph Job 95 will run and produce a table which goes to the Infograph and they produce laser printed output. That's how it works. The only reason 90 triggers 120 as far as I know is because when 90 finishes you want to run something else. A good idea isn't it? They're not logically connected. There's no business connection or file connection or anything like that. Its just when we have finished with that, fine. We've finished with Schedules, let's do something else. So it kicks off Instalment Billing which is 120, 122 and 125. So far as I know those are all IB. There's a curious little 100. The same reason again 125 kicks off 100 because that is not a bad idea. 120 – 120 if it doesn't work, so what. That's how it looks so you don't have to leave anything out. 122 – if 122 doesn't work we can't run 130, 135, 140, 145, 150. Those are the instalment billing reports. So those ones should be connected in. So far as I know there is no reason in the world why they can't actually come out of 122 and run next to it. 125 – there's a whole lot more reports. Those are all IB reports as well, except 220 and 225 update programs as far as I know. Yes, just flag batches again. That one also is flag batches. Then it generates piles and piles of reports down here somewhere.'
(Woolnough, M., 1988)

It is easy to see how difficult this interview would be to understand without some knowledge of the expert's task or purpose. This excerpt also shows how essential it is to understand the expert's personality. This expert, although he talked in an irreverent and glib way during the 'think aloud' interviews was also extremely diligent and direct in answering questions and in checking our knowledge. Additionally, how disjointed the whole process would become if the expert had to halt to explain every single concept and detail of his strategy.

The primary purposes of this interview technique are:

• to check specifically that the strategies the expert says are used really are the ones used when a problem is solved;
• to check the ordering of the sequence of the tasks, and the sources of information;
• to assist the elicitor in finding the cues that stimulate the expert's thoughts and in this way track down and follow the goal-directed behaviour of the expert.

The 'think aloud' interview in practice

The process is made easier if the expert is able to verbalize thoughts continuously. Sometimes however, experts get lost in their own thoughts and forget to speak. The elicitor must then gently bring the expert back so that the process again becomes public. Perhaps more difficult to deal with is the case where the expert jumps over particular parts, but appears to continue giving a continuous account of what is done. This shows particularly clearly why this exercise should be carried out later – it is more likely that the elicitor will notice such an omission in the expert's narrative because more is understood about the expert's practice, and be able to check the gap.

If the expert has skipped over a reasoning step, then the elicitor has to ask 'why' or 'what are you thinking about now'? The elicitor must follow the expert's reasoning closely and stop when there is a loss of continuity in the reasoning chain. After a few such interruptions, the expert usually gets the general idea and realizes that the elicitor really wants to know every thought, even if the expert believes they are trivial.

Problems using 'think aloud' interviewing

It can be difficult to simulate the expert's task in a useful way. The level of artificiality involved in constructing a set of circumstances suitable for the expert to talk about thought processes can be a problem. Often normal environmental conditions do not permit an interview set against a realistic background. It may not be possible to simulate the environment and therefore some degree of accuracy may have to be sacrificed. Nevertheless this interview is of sufficient importance to make it worth compensating for deficiencies or obstacles. The results are ultimately worthwhile because the 'think aloud' technique is less subject to bias and error. It is therefore essential as a last line of defence against error and misunderstanding.

• The elicitor may encounter a reluctant expert.

It is hard to verbalize while simultaneously thinking through a difficult problem, but the degree of difficulty can often be magnified by the personality of the expert, who might feel very uncomfortable with this process. The expert may feel exceptionally self-conscious, inhibited or irritated. If these feelings are very strong, it may not be possible to continue the interview without making some agreed modifications such as: a written component being used, or a role reversal exercise in which the elicitor attempts to solve the problem thinking aloud, and the expert listens, checks and, if necessary, corrects the elicitor's thinking. This is tedious and takes a lot of project time, it is not so useful as it sometimes seems at first to be as it sometimes deteriorates into a game for the expert, and so should be avoided unless absolutely necessary. Perhaps the expert could manage merely to describe what is done, and the elicitor could then come back to the thinking behind the actions as a separate stage.

Obviously the elicitor must work within whatever constraints arise from the particular project the elicitor is engaged in. The above suggestions are merely illustrative of the fact that it is nearly always possible, with a little thought beforehand, to modify techniques to suit circumstances.

• The elicitor can cause problems by being too intrusive.

The elicitor should not jump in too fast if the expert stops talking. If the expert has ceased to speak for a few moments, it can be really disconcerting to have someone interrupt your thoughts immediately. The expert may have just stopped to rest, or paused to collect some thoughts before speaking them aloud. It is even more disconcerting if the elicitor intrudes at every pause. Apart from occasional interventions, the elicitor wants the expert to keep the flow of information coming. Intrusion causes confusion and a disjointed record, it stops the expert thinking naturally and will most likely interfere with the elicitor's own understanding in later analysis.

• The act of talking aloud alters the expert's thinking processes.

As in many situations the act of consciously attending to a process can actually alter that process by adding a dimension that is not normally there (Bainbridge, L., 1979). It is a characteristic that cannot practically be avoided.

Reviewing the 'think aloud' interview

The elicitor is now working towards a final representation of the expertise. This is the time to integrate each of the domain views in relation to the whole. It is likely in the course of analysis of previous interviews that the elicitor has built a stronger mental schema of how the expertise fits together.

Reviewing the think aloud interview gives a chance to test the ideas in practice. It is sometimes beneficial to map out on paper, (or whiteboard) or in some graphical form: the step by step sequence of actions the expert performs, during problem solving activities, the flow of control in the expert's reasoning processes. The expert can then check through and either agree the sequence or alter it in some way.

4.4.4 The short review interview

This is often a sub-component of other interviews, where what has been covered before is checked back against the expert's understanding. The review is most often performed at the beginning of the next interview and because of the restraints of time, should be short and well structured. The expert should not need to provide large amounts of qualifying information in the review sessions. If he/she does, something was wrong with the original interview. Nevertheless, sometimes the expert is prompted after a long interval and while still fresh to bring up something which related to the material being reviewed. If this happens, make a note of it and assess its importance with respect to what has been established so far. Concentrate on the analysis of the previous interview, is it adequate?; accurate?; complete?

The review is not a full interview, and should not be allowed to change into one except where there is an obvious and urgent need, and both parties believe it necessary. Bear in mind that all the preparation and the mental set of the expert will be wasted by sudden changes of plan or shifts in direction. The review is for verifying knowledge already elicited, not to gain further knowledge.

5 Analysis

5.1 AN OUTLINE OF THE PROCESS OF ANALYSIS

5.1.1 Introduction

As the elicitor progresses through the interviews, and different aspects of the whole are explored in greater and greater depth, the analysis of each transcript provides a modular growth of understanding, as the elicitor's picture of the expert's knowledge is gradually incremented. Understanding is paced throughout the process by the successive views of the domain, right from the beginning generalities to final understanding.

The elicitor maintains control over the growth of information volume, and while there is no guarantee against redundancy or misconception without complete understanding, proper control ensures that any adverse effects from redundancy or minor error can be minimized. It is certainly unlikely that working ad-hoc would be more efficient unless by sheer luck.

Analysis begins before the interview starts. The examples below of interviews will illustrate this. What follows is an example of orientation interviewing. They are a pair of actual interviews on the same subject. The first one shows the best way to approach the expert and the interview itself in order to acquire information.

The second interview is also a real interview, but it is confused, and the interviewer has no purposeful intent. The result of any interview should conclude in a satisfactory amount of information elicited, in a form which lends itself to easy and speedy analysis. This implies that the information in the transcripts is in a concise and comprehensive form so that others, who were not present at the interview, can understand and use the knowledge it produces.

A

I   I hope you will agree to my tape recording this interview for accuracy. The tapes will be transcribed by myself and used as part of an evaluation report which will be given to Mr Adam and Ms Templer. The original tape I will keep and after transcription they will be over-recorded for some other interview. The transcripts will be shown to you for verification before the final copy is made. Do you agree to my using the tape recorder?

The expert now has the last word on whether a tape recorder is used, knowing who will have access to the tapes and what will become of them. This information should ease any concern connected with their use and in all probability the expert will allow the taping of the interview. It is essential however that you are sincere.

E   No, I don't mind.

I   I have been asked to take part in the evaluation of PRTD. As you have used it recently you must have several useful opinions about it so could you first tell me, how you came to use this shell?

This passage orientates the expert, she now knows the reasons for the interview (evaluation of the shell), an idea of what is wanted from her (opinions on the shell). The expert is orientated towards her reasons for using the shell. This helps in assessing what her frame of reference is when assessing the shell and will point up any biases that may arise

E   The A.I. group were looking for a shell or some means of rapid prototype expert systems, so that you could go to a user with a prototype and work out ideas from there. We looked at several very briefly, then we acquired PRTD for three months to evaluate. I had the job of, with SF, of investigating how good it was for our purpose.

This reply clearly shows exactly why this shell was chosen, the purpose of the investigation and the criteria of the assessment, i.e. 'how good is it for rapid prototyping'.

I   What is PRTD?

This question will provide an introduction for any prospective reader of the transcripts who is not familiar with the reasons for the assessment or what PRTD is.

E It is an expert system shell, or what PRTD the producers of it
   call an advice language. It's a high level language which
   allows you to format rules to make a rule based system. It
   provides you with the rule formats and all the manipulation
   of rules necessary. You write the rules in that according to
   syntax they specify. It's used very much like a programming
   language, you have to compile it. You edit your program first
   of all, then you compile it, then you run it. You have a run
   time session; it then works through the rules. Its not like
   some of the shells where it uses some English language-like
   format.

   *As requested the expert gives a high level description of the shell which
   provides the interviewer with a base for further knowledge and appraisal.*

I Do you need any special skills to run PRTD?

   *This question discloses how easy it is to use the shell. The sentence was
   phrased this way so not to receive the expert's personal views, because as an
   expert she would have found it easy, and may not have voiced her pre-
   learning views.*

E You need to get your knowledge in, in some form, therefore
   you need a knowledge engineer to do the knowledge engineering process. I think it needs programming skills to use
   the language because it doesn't have an English-like format.
   You've got to know the syntax, and you've got to know the
   control structure of it. It's got a fairly messy control
   structure.

I Do you need to know any A.I. techniques?

   *This question is a prompt question, i.e. I require more knowledge about
   this please.*

E I think it helps, because then you know what it is trying to
   do. Their documentation is a reference guide, it doesn't have
   a user guide. In fact they do suggest that you go on their 4-
   day course first of all. I think if you were new to it you would
   need to go on their course. It took sometime to work out how
   it worked just by using their documentation.

I How did you use PRTD, what knowledge did you put in it?

   *This question requires the expert to reveal her specific use of the shell. It
   should reveal how the shell applied itself to the exercise. Then it is possible
   to compare skill with use.*

E What we were looking for was something where very little

knowledge engineering was needed. Therefore where rules were more or less in a form that we could use at the end. So wha; we did for this was to take one of the expert books on plant diseases, and we took knowledge about tomatoes for that, which was a very trivial task, but the main purpose really was to see how easy the PRTD shell was to use, not to stretch its capabilities.

This answer prompts the next question.

I   How easy was PRTD to use?

E   The documentation was lacking in overall explanations, you had to work out what the system did by reading lists of syntactical constructs in the language. It was easy enough if you had a programming background, I think if you didn't it would be difficult to use, unless you went on their course. I think that would be OK, then you could get on with it quite well. But given the reference guide and the software and without a bit of experience you will be at odds.

I   Do you think it fulfilled the function it set out to fulfil?

Asking for a clarification of why the explanations already given are related to one of the functions of the interview (prototype use).

E   I think it does because they don't claim very much for it, they don't claim that it will solve every single problem you have. They call it an advice language and tell you what kind of system you can build using it, and it can certainly do that kind of thing; to build a diagnostic type knowledge based system. What it gives you then is the possibility of using probabilities, and the ability to build a rule based system. The other things it has, compared with other previous versions of other expert systems shells, is that it can interfere with data-bases and view data; it's generally more friendly with the outside world.

I   What were your first impressions of it?

This question quizzes the expert for an opinion and it gives the expert the opportunity to 'open up' a little and say something about what she liked and didn't like about the shell.

E   We didn't look at many expert system shells. Compared with some of the others it was more flexible, you had more variety of constructs within it, different types of rules. But having looked at others they may turn out to be more useful if we had looked at the more expensive, more flexible shells. The main disadvantage I think really was they needed to be programmed, complied, debugged and run. Doing it on a PC was quite slow, but that was partly to do with the PC's lack of editing or any other possible programming tools, the lack of any programming tools.

and another prompt question.

I   Were there any other problems that you found? etc. . .

Looking at the transcript itself you can see that the questions are short and to the point and that the answers ample and in accord with the question. This is how it should be in the first few interviews where the interviewer and expert require some structure to achieve orientation and a base on which to progress.

The elicitor should intrude as little as possible with the expert's informative flow. The expert can therefore gain momentum and is mindful of the task of contributing information, which can be achieved in their characteristic way.

B

The interview that follows is also taken from an actual interview. Note that there is no introduction and no indication of what information is required from the expert.

I   Does WERT stand for anything?
E   No, It's just a word representing something.
I   I thought that would probably be it. No, I was going to ask if there has been a new release of WERT since the documentation we had available since the one we have, April and June, if so what are its most remarkable features?

What is the expert to make of this?, is he to answer the question he now knows he was going to be asked? Also how is the expert to know what the interviewer may mean by 'remarkable' (remarkably different from the last release one would have to suppose, but this does not add to your knowledge).

E   No, its an on-going package.
I   What are the hardware requirements, and how portable is it?

More than one question. Usually a person who is asked several or embedded questions will reply to the first or the last question only, this expert manages to answer both questions, but in reverse order.

E   WERT is written in Pascal, specifically for its portability. Although if you want it on a machine which is outside of our range, it still takes us 2 months to port it. It runs presently on the range of VAXs down to the PC variety, to other intermediate machines.

The obvious question to ask would be: what exactly is the range, this would supply a useful criteria of the machine ranges.

I   So the environmental software requirements are that there is a version of Pascal available?

E   It has to be a fairly comprehensive version of Pascal – we can port it to other versions, but it does take longer and we can add man months if it's Pascal.

What exactly does the expert mean by comprehensive. Could he not be asked to list the acceptable (comprehensible?) ones, as opposed to the 'others' and how many man-months extra will the 'others' take?

I   You, presumably, having developed it yourselves are the only organization to market it.

Why not simply ask 'who markets the product' without the insinuation.

E   Strictly yes, apart from the WERT, which you have to buy through WERT.

I   I was going to ask how much memory does its various parts require. The executive, presumably resides in memory. Something I wasn't quite clear about was the. . . . Tuh, tuh, tuh . . . I can't quite remember what you call it. . . . What we might call the knowledge base. The rules themselves, after compilation, they are shunted out to back-up aren't they, they are written to disk?

E   Uh, the rules? may. . .

The expert is beginning to lose hope of being actively involved in this interview. Which of the many questions or implied questions does the expert answer?

I   Not the executive, presumably they will have to reside in memory.

E   Well it's split strictly into separate parts, into executive and compiler. You need one in memory at one time. OK. The compiler like any compiler just produces a norm, sort of. . .

The expert is trying hard to get back to the interview.

I   Yes, but when you have compiled the rules, you can forget the compiler, can't you, when you are actually running the thing. The executive will reside in memory, and I have the impression that the compiler wrote the rules to disk. I have a feeling that they fetched them one at a time, or in chunks. How is that managed?

The interviewer seems to know more about the subject than the expert and is complicating the issue by forcing the expert into substantiating what the interviewer knows or thinks he knows. If the interviewer answers his own questions this has the effect of reducing expert participation and the interviewer's comments will supplant the expert's contribution to the interview, therefore there is less knowledge in the interview and in consequence there is less to analyse.

The interview continues. . .

I   What sort of support do you provide? Do you provide things like consistency, courses, things like that afterwards for your package purchase?

E   For your package you get a compiler and executive. For all other machines other than your PC you get a day's person's time to help you install it.

The questions have not been fully answered but the interviewer carries on nevertheless.

I   Perhaps this is an insulting question. I don't think I shall ask that.
Ha. Ha.
No that's redundant, (looking down a list).
How long has it been on the market as a product. A couple of years or longer? (scratching noises as the question on the list is scratched out).

E   About 2 years.

'About' can mean before 2 years or after 2 years, this could make quite a difference if we knew the point of the question.

I   OK, what order of magnitude have, how many packages have you installed?

E   I'm not sure. Uh . . . around about under a magnitude of around 100, average.

Total confusion now, the expert has lost all direction and is now even using the interviewer's meaningless phraseology.
An average derived from what measure?

The interviewer is now reading down a list and is apparently not interested in the answer.
What is the interviewer trying to find out, is it, indirectly, an attempt to uncover how much expertise the expert has? The expert may interpret the question this way too.

I   (reading) Ah, now this is interesting. The introduction also states that the executives can be used in batch or interactive mode. What's all this batch thing?

E   Well it's. . .

The interviewer does not allow the expert to answer.

I   So, the point being that the executive provides you with some kind of, in that instance, graphical information concerning the behaviour hybrid systems, so that you can go back and tweak it to find it yourself.

The interviewer is making his own implicit confusion explicit during the interview by asking the expert to clarify items in his own mind. The expert is asked to act as a mediator to fill in the missing bits or to confirm the interviewer's views. This is not what an elicitation interview is for, and it is, in this context, not the task of the expert.

E   Histograms, rather than fine tuning. No, I don't think so. It's my personal opinion. . .

I   But essentially . . . etc, etc. . .

The interviewer completely ignores the expert's personal opinion, a source of many useful 'truths', and effectively deprives the expert of all motivation to take further part in the interview.

We do not know for what purpose Interview B is held and therefore what knowledge is required. The interview is in effect almost totally squandered, except as an example of bad interviewing. The interviewer's reason for asking particular questions is not made explicit (Berry, D., 1987). Therefore the amount of knowledge contained in the transcript is extremely low. The expert will probably not be willing to take part in such an interview again and the interviewer commented: 'I couldn't get going with this expert, he was unwilling to tell me much!'

We have seen many transcripts similar to this one. They are useless as sources of information and they are impossible to analyse. The main mistake that elicitors make is to interview in an ad-hoc way; not planning the content of the interview before interviewing, so the interviewer jumps from item and subject to subject, pro-

gressively thinking of questions to ask. The interview is conse-
quently disjointed and the content cannot be followed constructively
in later analysis.

The expert too is not orientated in any particular direction, so the
answers are not triggering sections of information in the way they
could be. The expert has to predict what might follow, and not being
prepared for the sort of questions or subject areas may affect the
expert's motivation as well as failing to activate memory.

Another grave mistake is not making the plan for the interview
explicit in the question, so that the expert can answer the question
directly and the transcripts can be analysed in the light of knowing
exactly *what* the question is and exactly *why* it was asked, ie, what
information is sought and for what purpose?

Cost and the time must also be considered when we judge the
benefits we expect from the transcript. It is costly to transcribe tapes
with an assortment of dialogue but very little information contained
in them. It is also time consuming and wearying to toil through non-
essential, trivial material. Good interviewing will get results quickly.
The information gathered can then be analysed without difficulty.
The interviewer then has a willing expert who knows time will not
be wasted.

5.1.2 Analysing the transcript

At the end of each interview session the elicitor possesses a
transcript of raw information which must then be analysed in depth.
Some superficial analysis may also have been done during the
interview, while asking questions and probing the expert, but this is
limited by the need to concentrate on the interview itself, and
further limited by the amount of information that can be understood
after just one hearing. Nevertheless, because the session has been
recorded the elicitor can take time to review the interview as many
times as necessary, fully exploring and understanding it.

The final process of putting together the results of the analysis
sessions, should result in a model of the expert's knowledge and
function within the domain. Whether engineered into an expert
system, or preserved as an archive, it constitutes an essential
document, and can be used repeatedly for:

• reference,
• checking information
• updating or modifying a system, or the knowledge itself.

5.1.3 Using a log

It is a useful habit for the elicitor to keep a log of the process of elicitation, an informal supplement to the required documentation. This is essentially a personal document, it constitutes a very unofficial reference point during and after the elicitation process.

The elicitor records various thoughts about the project as a whole, the interview sessions and any progress so far. Impressions, ideas and speculations which would be out of place in the normal documentation can be recorded in the log and can provide a yardstick of the elicitor's growing understanding. This can add immeasurably to the learning process both within a given project and, more generally, when teaching the elicitation skills.

5.1.4 First reading of the transcript

We have argued that despite the cost involved of recording verbatim transcripts of each interview, the value of a permanent record of the expert's actual words easily justifies any extra outlay. This record can be referred to again and again, and functions as a safety net against many of the potential pitfalls we have discussed so far. Whichever form the interview transcript takes, whether notes, verbatim transcript, or questionnaire, it must now be subject to careful scrutiny and interpretation.

This process is subdivided into three phases. Each phase used to extract a different type of information:

- a first phase to get the feel of the result and do some essential classification;
- the second phase to enact the more formal aspects of analysis;
- the third to examine emergent problems, fresh information or questions for the expert.

Phase one overview

During the first phase, the elicitor seeks the major concepts, procedure descriptions and expert heuristics. At the same time the elicitor gets a feeling for the knowledge elicited so far: Is it simple or complex? Does it appear to fit together well or are there gaps? Are there any questions which immediately demand attention?, and so on. This first pass provides an opportunity to soften up the transcript for the more detailed analysis coming next.

The first pass should not take up a great deal of time assuming that proper segmentation into Domain Views, and complexity layering have been carried out according to the guidelines in Chapter One.

The ability to speed read is a useful additional skill, allowing faster processing of information while maintaining adequate comprehension. In addition the elicitor may also examine the transcript for implicit information about the expert, revealed by the answers. Such information might influence the elicitor's thinking and planning for the immediate or longer term. If the expert had a decided preference for assessing numerical data when solving problems for instance, this information might be usefully fed back into later questioning strategy and verification procedures.

Phase two overview

The second phase consists of a more formal analysis of the transcript: actively looking for knowledge and structuring it into important component aspects: domain, task and problem, etc. Use different coloured marker pens to mark out each required category of information. Concepts in the same class, for example, can be marked with a particular colour, allowing quick identification of concept classes. Obviously this can present problems if there are a large number of different classes to be demarcated, then the elicitor must rely on ingenuity. The essential thing is to devise some way consistently to highlight things of interest. The advantage of colour is simply that reference to any particular category of information is instantly visible, using a colour key. A glance at the pages of the transcript can 'pull out' various different information particles that the elicitor seeks.

If the elicitor has the use of a multi-window workstation or computer the transcript can be read and the salient points can be copied on to an analysis window, picking out concepts, say, in capital letters, for easier identification. Thus different cuts can be made across the information in the transcript each represented in a window on that aspect (metaphorically and literally).

Once the information can be easily identified, the elicitor is ready to begin interpreting it. Such as building concept dictionaries, databases, examine relationships and interdependencies, the flow of information and the ways the expert controls it. These aspects will be examined in much greater detail below.

Phase three overview

The third and last phase consists of formulating any important questions or points to be clarified, analysing any new or unexpected information and identifying any actual or potential problems. Generally, problems might arise from:

- The knowledge itself, which does not seem to cohere: doubts, ambiguities, or apparent inconsistencies.
- Potential system development problems, that is: problems translating the current practices of the expert into system equivalents.
- The elicitation process itself where communication has apparently failed between expert and elicitor, scheduling difficulties, sudden unexpected occurrences which interfere with the elicitation process.

The earlier a problem is spotted the less the actual damage will result, and the less the potential for other indirectly or directly related problems.

5.1.5 Using a data dictionary

A data dictionary is a store of descriptions and definitions of knowledge which is held on the computer. It is a valuable device for recording information on concepts, relationships, facts and their origin, meanings and current use (Sturzda, P., 1983).

The database expands as knowledge is gathered, developed and integrated. Objects of interest should be documented in the data dictionary and accompanied by a definition, which clearly states both the meaning, and the context in which that object may be found. Such documentation of all the information gathered in each interview must be kept throughout all the stages of the system's development, since subsequent developments may decree that some areas of the knowledge are developed more fully or have an alteration of use, for instance.

The Data dictionary constitutes the bare bones of the knowledge, formed by the definitions of the words the expert uses. Sometimes it is useful to add the interview number as a reference marker, indicating at what stage the concept was discussed. Later reference to this concept can then be traced back to the original transcript quickly and efficiently should questions or problems arise.

The benefits of using a data dictionary are:

1. Better communication with the expert, engineer and users.
2. Controlling the knowledge elements in a simple and effective way.
3. Ability to change, introduce new knowledge.
4. Reduce knowledge redundancy and inconsistency.
5. Determine the impact of changes to the knowledge.
6. Centralizing the elements of knowledge as an aid to the knowledge base design and in expanding the design and use.

The elicitor may wish to extend the scope of the data dictionary, so that it becomes a knowledge dictionary containing knowledge about:

- facts
- concepts
- procedures
- dependencies
- relationships
- conflicts
- ambiguities and their resolutions

together with any other relevant factors, perhaps even information on authorization and security codes, tables, measures, etc.

It should be noted however that a data dictionary has to be maintained and the costs of updating and maintaining can be high. This must be weighed against the potential benefits, especially in large integrated systems where there are many users with potentially divergent needs or views of the domain, or there is the likelihood of later system expansion or development.

5.2 ANALYSIS AND UNDERSTANDING

It is possible that a full understanding of the expertise may not occur until well into the process of elicitation. The larger and more complex the domain, the more pronounced this effect. This presents a major challenge to the elicitor: remaining calm, secure and reasonably confident even though comprehension of the whole picture is lost for some time.

It is perfectly reasonable for a practitioner to feel insecure about lacking understanding. Most people can recapture the feelings of helplessness and bafflement at the prospect of tackling a large field of human knowledge for the first time, and receiving large amounts of as yet unintegrated information (Brobrow, E., 1975). When this is compounded with deadlines and time limitations arising from resource constraints, the inevitable fears emerge:

> *'Will it all make sense in time?'*
> *'This is too much for me to take on by myself'*

and worse:

> *'I think I'm drowning in it or going mad'*
> *'Have I got what it takes to learn quickly enough?'*

In fact, not to feel some of these things might suggest a lack of sensitivity to the problems of elicitation; not to admit to them, lack of honesty, or worse than both of these, just overconfidence, underlying the inability to face reality. It is too easy to be sceptical about the significance of these fears when not faced with them immediately, and too easy to make light of it afterwards.

Over and above the specific function of any recommendation we make in this book, our intention has also been to enhance confidence by ensuring control. But control cannot guarantee comprehension, nor prevent the harmful effects that panic could have. For instance, if the elicitor prematurely imposed interpretation on the expert's knowledge and rushed ahead with the machine implementation (which is a more familiar method of control), there is a possibility of missing vital and subtle elements of another ordering that the expert has been trying to put across.

We have already noted that skill in elicitation necessitates temperamental adjustments. The elicitor must learn to live with incomplete information and a partial understanding until late in the process. There is little else to recommend other than self-discipline. This is a factor that should influence the judgement of those concerned with selecting candidates to train as knowledge elicitors. The evidence, particularly when observing trainees, suggests that this is one of the most difficult things to live with.

The process of continued concentration on a particular domain ensures that some understanding begins to grow. Even though the elicitor may not be aware of it, there is some settling and subconscious processing of information going on in the mind, in the background. Despite the fact that we may not consciously understand the emerging pattern of knowledge, that doesn't stop our minds from working on the problem it presents (Chase, W., 1973). It is this invisible maturation process which often leads to sudden leaps of understanding as things suddenly fit together. It follows that we should respect and trust the invisible work of our minds and not attempt to force the pace of understanding unnecessarily.

Some systems have required little on-going documentation because of 'it's got to be built yesterday' time-scales. It is very enticing to forge ahead without needing to document all you have done and indeed to carry on with all projects in this way. This method may seem to be good (at first) for you but confusing to everyone else.

5.3 INTERPRETING THE RESULTS OF TRANSCRIPT ANALYSIS

Most transcript information will require interpreting, a process of information selection and refinement, compressing the knowledge into a form where we can begin to formulate a suitable interim representation. We shall examine: (1) interpretation of the transcript, and (2) representation of the knowledge.

5.3.1 Interpretation

Having identified and isolated the major concepts in the expert's domain, using the procedures outlined above, and elicitor must now examine them carefully, both in their own right and in the context of mutual inter-dependencies and relationships displayed within the conceptual organization of the knowledge.

Since it is also important that the expert and elicitor agree about what constitutes the correct interpretation of the knowledge, this must be done in a concrete and publicly representable way, not least because any future system design will be based on this agreed conceptual scheme. It will often be necessary for that representation to be transparent to others, outside of the domain itself, as well as other experts. The final representation must therefore be in a public form that any party could understand. Ideally then, it would appear that the final representation should be cast in already existing and well understood representation formalisms, such as those used elsewhere in systems analysis. We shall argue below that this is not always the case.

5.3.2 Conceptual analysis

What is it?

What does conceptual analysis involve? When we examine a concept we need to know, in more precise terms than normal, what it means, how it is used in this particular context, and whether there is any variation in understanding, or use, by different experts within the domain (Sloman, A., 1978). Too much variation of this kind could affect the possibility of system development, though difficulties of this kind should normally emerge at the feasibility stage.

The elicitor needs to know about any presuppositions or assumptions that the expert makes, which will affect the application of a particular concept, and what boundaries are implicit for the scope of its use in the domain.

Everyday versus specialized use

Many concepts which have everyday meanings may also have a specialized meaning or application within a given knowledge domain. Take for example the concept of 'tension'. To a mechanical engineer it has a particular and fairly precise meaning. Not the same as might be understood in a medical context which is closer to, though not necessarily the same as, our everyday understanding of the word. Similarly, with 'stress', or 'pressure'.

Conceptual relationships

Similarly, the concepts used within a domain may exhibit different relationships from one another within a specialized knowledge domain, when compared with the relationships encountered in everyday use. This can be a more subtle source of confusion and error. Concepts do not always fall into neatly divided or easily discernible groups. Often we are dealing with 'families' of concepts (Wittgenstein) where the connections and similarities are more diffuse and harder to identify and explain.

A familiar example is that of games: football, chess and 'hide and seek' seem to have little in common even though we classify them all as a form of game. If we attempt to classify the three under the heading 'sport' the apparent relationship is less clear: football is a sport, chess we would not normally call sport, though it is played in tournaments which bear many of the familiar hallmarks of a sporting competition, and hide and seek is not a sport in any normal sense of the term.

In much the same way, relationships between concepts in an experts domain may have crucial shifting relationships or resemblances that are not apparent to the layman.

Classification of concepts

It is also worth observing that many conceptual taxonomies are a matter of convenience as much as of necessity. A conceptual classification may depend on what purpose the expert is intending them to serve (Sowa, J., 1968, 1981). This may not necessarily stay the same at all times; the expert may have a more dynamic conception of conceptual roles. It is also worth noting that the expert might still talk about the concepts as if they were part of a static hierarchy, and quite possibly may not even be aware of the full subtlety of the conceptual scheme.

The elicitor must tread carefully as always and bear in mind what kinds of assumptions are brought to the task. Concept definition and boundaries are relative, certainly to context, frequently to intention of use and, less frequently, to time. Yet it is common to find concepts and their relationships used as if they were, at worst, fixed and immutable truths, at best, well defined and fixed reference points capable always of precise definition. It may be true that there exist very stable and well defined concepts (but probably fewer than most people suppose), especially where we have historically assigned such values, as in the case of scientific definitions for example. However this kind of agreement is far less likely in an expert domain, especially if the knowledge domain is fairly new.

Conceptual distortion

The dangers of misinterpretation should not be underestimated because of the profound effect they can have on any project. A small distortion of meaning can ripple through a system, becoming more magnified over time. It is like a wrong value in a calculation. A small error in some relatively minor part of the computation can repeat and magnify itself in many subsequent calculations, resulting in a far more significant error by the end of the process.

Nevertheless this kind of error must be carefully distinguished from the change of meaning imposed by the elicitor for the sake of system development. It is often true that the very process of acquiring, representing and encoding knowledge will result in some, frequently necessary, loss of conceptual richness, but this process should be consciously controlled and any such reduction should be worked out in advance by the elicitor and expert.

It is also possible that a machine representation needs more knowledge than the human expert would normally require, so it is usual to go back to the expert and work out what knowledge is necessary to plug that particular gap.

Two checkpoints

• Does the interpreted information reflect a coherent and correct account (for the purpose of system building) in its explicit form?
• Does everyone agree that it does?

Always make sure you have checked; it's always the one detail the elicitor doesn't check.

Examples

It is easy to underestimate subtle nuances of difference and classify two concepts as the same as one another. It is worth being wary of synonyms. In a case where there is a word which apparently does the same work as another, the replacement may bring important and subtle variations to bear elsewhere in the domain, there may be an obscure but important variance in the work. There is a subtle difference between 'estimate' and 'forecast' for instance, yet they can be used, properly or not, as synonyms in some contexts. We don't often refer to weather estimation.

Consider the degree of difference between 'large', 'big', 'great', 'sizeable', 'grand', and 'substantial'. In some cases, where the granularity of the knowledge is coarse and we do not need to consider much detail, there may be no necessity to consider subtle discriminations, but with systems requiring finer levels of detail, the degree of synonymity declines.

Conceptual analysis in the context of expert communities requires precise understanding of application and use (even if not always conscious). A proper analysis of similarities and differences between the various concepts can be of substantial benefit, even when no formal quantification is required. For this sort of situation, Repertory Grid Technique (Easterby-Smith, M., 1981) can be a valuable tool. We shall briefly look at this and other tools which the elicitor might find useful later in this chapter (section 5.5.1).

5.3.3 Task analysis

Experts usually apply their knowledge to an overall task within a domain. There are various types of tasks: diagnosis, planning or prediction for example. Thus the interview transcript can be analysed in terms of the overall task the expert performs. This high level task can often be broken down into sub-component tasks, each of which can be analysed separately. The knowledge and procedures required for the execution of each sub-task can then be isolated, and, if required, any mapping of common elements across sub-tasks or even sub-domains (Chandrasekaran, B., 1987) or their respective procedures, and any critical interdependencies defined and worked out.

During both the Outline and the Structured interviews (the first and second phase interview techniques), the expert will probably have touched on the sub-tasks and procedures used to fulfil any functions within the domain. Now the elicitor, having by this time already established a feeling for the domain knowledge and, during previous analysis, established the conceptual framework within which the expert works, can begin to construct a picture of the component sub-tasks and procedures used, and the way they fit together when the expert carries out any functions within the domain.

Analysis of tasks is often helped by making diagrams, preferably on a white board, so that it is easy to change dependencies, knowledge inputs and outputs, and so on. There will also be enough space to develop analysis of a task within a particular scoping of it. The analysis can be formally drawn later. Seeing the task in a visual form often prompts the elicitor (and the expert) to spot what is missing in the analysis (Davies, R., 1983) and further helps to guide the overall elicitation.

We are looking for verbal cues such as:

'I do this here because . . .'

suggesting that there is a test or procedure to establish a result,

'Knowing this I move to this aspect . . .'

suggesting that one task, out of several possibilities will be suggested by certain conditions, and so on.

Reading between the lines

When analysing interview texts it is sometimes equally important to look out for what is not said (or even implied) as at what is. We have already noted that even though the expert is trying really hard consciously to enunciate every step of thinking, the expert fuses parts together into natural units of action (natural to the expert at least). The elicitor must spot these units which must be properly understood for system building, and further decompose them into smaller basic steps or sub-procedures.

Remember that even in what is apparently simple there is often hidden complexity: it is like the now familiar analogy of describing how to make coffee step by step and then turning it into an algorithm: the high level human description misses out many of the essential but boringly obvious details:

Task Description: 'fill the kettle'.

Algorithm: Pick up the kettle: take off lid: put under the tap: turn on the tap, etc.

The level of detail required by the elicitor for the system may vary (often referred to as the knowledge granularity) depending on:

• the final goal of elicitation;
• the degree of sophistication of the final system;
• the requirements of the users;

and so on.

It is also likely that the elicitor will have to analyse the transcripts for the unstated, then match up and fill out the task performance with the necessary knowledge.

Task execution

By the time the elicitor has got to the stage of conducting 'think aloud' interviews, towards the end of the elicitation, the outcome from previous interviewing phases will be used (Outline and Structured interviewing) to construct these 'think aloud' scenarios. The elicitor should then know enough about the expert's task and its constituent parts to construct revealing cases or sub-tasks for the expert to run through. The actual execution of real or simulated tasks enables the elicitor to piece together a model of the expert's problem solving behaviour which can then be emulated on a machine (Berry, D., 1984).

Note it is necessary that the machine should arrive at the same conclusions as the expert when it is given a problem to solve, but it is not necessary that the system should emulate the exact behaviour of the expert, merely that it should be as consistent and accurate as the expert.

The elicitor can finally construct the results of the task analysis into some procedural formalism: a procedural flow chart, or a diagram of action states, a transcript of task execution in action or whatever best fits the particular context. The elicitor should now be able to state for any particular task:

- what information is required at what point;
- what form it must take;
- what alternative information may be necessary for a task.

The elicitor can then start to think about realistically partitioning the knowledge and can begin to look at what sort of machine formalism will best represent the flavour of the expert's knowledge in action. The result of the task analysis should enable the elicitor to construct a description which illustrates point by point what steps are involved in the execution of the expert's role and represent the structure of the sub-tasks and the expert's problem-solving behaviour. If we use part of the same transcript for a small example of the 'think aloud' interview (Chapter 4, page 113) we can see how it is done.

An excerpt of a 'think aloud' interview:

'The only reason 90 triggers 120 as far as I know is because when 90 finishes you want to run something else'

As far as I know. This may just be an expression of ignorance, a flippant remark or a gloss over of some essential knowledge. Check which it is.

'They are not logically connected'.

Logically connected. It looks as though this means a business connection or a file connection and something else may be included. Check this and whether there are other types of connections and what their significances are.

'There is no business connection or file connection or anything like that.'

Business connection. What is the connection specifically between 90 and 120 or between any other job and what are they?

File connection. The same as above, and is there more?

'We've finished with Schedules, lets do something else. So it kicks off Instalment Billing which is 120, 122.'

Schedules
Instalment Billing

Why did Schedules run before Instalment Billing? Is there some signifi-cance in the placing of jobs? Is there some overall strategy, or is it permissible to run the schedule by running individual jobs, i.e. some Schedules and then some Instalment Billing?

'and 125. So far, as I know, they are all IB, etc'

So far as I know. The expert had a frequent habit of answering flippantly. We always had to check if (unless it was obvious) he was implying that he really doesn't know they are all IBs or has he not checked that they are all IBs.

In the small excerpt above, issues concerning the overall strategy and the associated procedures are noted, as well as any information not known previously.

- The important words can be placed automatically into a knowledge dictionary and the appropriate explanations can follow as soon as the expert supplies that information. Information can be added to Schedules and Instalment Billing as they should already exist in a knowledge dictionary.
- All nouns, if they are not known already, must be investigated and their meanings understood.
- All expressions about the boundaries of knowledge must be investigated, i.e. this may be so, as far as I know, sometimes I know, etc.
- Anything which starts or finalizes an action, or an intermediate action must be investigated, i.e. now, later, do, can't do, finished, let's do, etc.

5.4 REPRESENTING THE KNOWLEDGE

5.4.1 Why build a representation of the knowledge?

Wellbank argues that to maintain the enthusiasm of the expert (Wellbank, M., 1983): 'Get something working quickly. Nii (1983) suggests that there should be a system for the expert to see in a matter of days rather than weeks.'

Under the circumstances where one is dealing with a particularly unenthusiastic or sceptical expert this may well be good advice, though whether the idea that an inadequate machine representation will really prompt the expert to suggest 'improvements', or confirm some of their worst fears, is open to debate.

We stress the practice of building a model before considering implementation wherever this is practicable. This may seem like a luxury. Some practitioners are not able to, or not allowed to, nor can afford it. Nevertheless, we believe it should be the case wherever possible.

Obviously, this does not preclude experimentation and trial of ideas using machines: it would be naive to expect that no machine modelling or experimentation with machine formalisms would be necessary. However, there is a substantial difference between this and the rather wasteful ad-hoc prototyping approach, where computational considerations push thoughtful elicitation procedures into the background.

Under the ad-hoc scheme as soon as any understanding of the expertise is gained, the first prototype begins. It may be possible that on some occasions, where the information volume is low and the knowledge relatively simple, practitioners may get away with this. But there are many pitfalls. For instance, what if, at a late stage, knowledge emerges which changes or invalidates the initial assumptions? The first prototype is either scrapped or significant time and resources used to modify it, and we begin again. This might happen more than once. Where there is a commitment to unlimited experiment, a large budget and few constraints on time, this may be acceptable though it still seems wasteful. How many companies can afford, as Nii poetically puts it, to: 'count on throwing drafts away, like a writer or a painter'.

In a commercial environment, especially a competitive one, writers and painters tend to be scarce and those that exist find survival difficult. So would any practitioner, we suspect, who was employed to develop commercial systems, if they adopted this attitude to company resources (Woods, A., 1983). This is why the elicitation should be completed first, at least to a degree in which the knowledge is fairly well understood. It doesn't guarantee that the model once designed, will then automatically be straightforward to implement, but it is unlikely to require quite so many 'drafts' to achieve the right effect.

It also means that planning, choosing and costing the hard- and software requirements can be done in the light of substantial information. This could prove a considerable economic advantage, to add to those economies already made through use of concentrated, controlled elicitation. Needless to say there is the hidden potential saving of not requiring potentially costly prototypes.

5.4.2 Conventional versus non-standard representation techniques?

The knowledge representation should be adequate and intelligible to all parties, for instance:

- someone not engaged in the project;
- a future practitioner who is to update or extend the knowledge or a system based upon it;
- an interested non-specialist, such as a manager, or colleagues from different business areas.

There may be difficulties inherent in representing the knowledge, however: it might not lend itself well to a clear semi-English rule formulation, or to conventional representation – such as flow charts or decision trees. There may be a genuine case for a seemingly more 'organic' representation, which attempts to reflect what is unique and not to squeeze the expertise into a predetermined shape.

Yet it has already been argued (Morik, K., 1987) that these conventional techniques are more transparent because well understood and well documented. Anyone can understand them if they understand the formalism, or find out by reference to the documentation, if they don't.

Non-standard representation may not be so well documented, may be misleading or unclear to outsiders or worse, may become incomprehensible if the author is no longer available to explain it. There is a tendency for non-standard representations to be cryptic, particularly in diagramatic forms, despite the best intentions of their authors. Also they tend to proliferate, there being potentially as many ways to represent things as there are things to represent, or at least, people to make the attempt. Finally it is often argued, more contentiously, that all non-standard representations actually do the same work that conventional techniques are quite capable of doing.

This last point can be countered by arguing that current representation techniques, such as flow diagrams and borrowings from data modelling, which are frequently used, were originally developed with another, perhaps less sophisticated set of requirements in mind. Yet in practice these techniques frequently require qualitative changes to make them suitable for use in capturing the subtlety and complexity of domain expertise.

Perhaps it is necessary to preserve this distinction between using non-standard representation techniques for developing one's own understanding, and their use in formal modelling and representation. But is the argument for this, adequate grounds to overlook the case for extending the semantics of representation for knowledge elicitation and knowledge based systems? Perhaps there is a compromise.

5.4.3 A compromise solution?

Obviously where a traditional and well understood representation can encompass the knowledge it makes sense to use it, so long as care is taken to ensure that minimal distortion of the knowledge takes place. There are a large range of tried and tested techniques which have proved invaluable: rules, decision and hierarchy trees, graphs, state transition diagrams and so on.

A suggestion is to reduce the transcripts to the barest minimum, showing only the essential knowledge. This not only conveys a 'sense' of the domain, which promotes understanding, but also gives the knowledge engineer as much or as little information as is required. The expert can control the amount and at the same time the speed at which it can be retained. Another method is to include the engineer in some of the 'think aloud' interviews, after becoming accustomed to some of the technical details of the domain, in this way acquiring knowledge and achieving a 'feel' for the way the expert thinks and works. These form the basis of understanding from which discussions of machine representation can be attained.

The accumulation of information from the elicitor for implementation purposes is usually characteristic of the individual engineer. Discussions between the elicitor and engineer are essential so that the elicitor can supply the information required in a suitable form.

There may be occasions when it is simply not possible to use these techniques without doing considerable violence to the knowledge. In these cases, though admittedly very rare, it may be perfectly reasonable to modify conventional techniques, or even invent another more adequate system. What must be the case is that the conventions of such changes or inventions must be absolutely clear and explicit in a comprehensively documented form. It should be made explicit what has been modified and why.

Whether everyone agrees with the case for such measures is a matter for the politics of the context in which individual practitioners work. What matters is that the change can be comprehended and the result is accurate and faithful to the original knowledge.

Generally it would seem wise to resort to non-standard representation only as a last resort, and keep such changes to a minimum. Only dire necessity should be the mother of invention.

On the other hand practitioners should not underestimate the dangers of distortion and impoverishment of meaning which might result from transferring old, well established techniques designed for service in another, possibly less demanding context. The dangers of semantic impoverishment are real.

5.4.4 Other requirements of representation

1. The representation of knowledge should be jointly agreed among the expert, elicitor, engineer (if different) and the users.
2. It should be easy to update.
3. It should be modular, accurate and complete.

Machine formalisms

The way the knowledge is represented in order to understand it may not be the same as a machine formalism (Schank, R., 1977; Michalski, R., 1980). Thus another level of abstraction away from the expert's conception may be entailed. Such a machine formalism will probably be based on one of, or a mixture of, the three most prevalent forms: rules, frames and semantic nets.

It would be extremely unwise to set down rules directly from a transcript. The knowledge usually has to be ordered in some way so that the rule will function according to what is required of it. If a rule, such as in a scheduling system, says, *if the As are finished, then start the Bs*, this may not be very useful, or necessarily correct in all situations. What would be useful is a list of 'jobs' that must be done in sequence, the reasons why they must be done in that order and the constraints that may occur. The engineer can then represent this knowledge in the way that is appropriate given the overall design of the system.

Rules may be appropriate in several different situations and then only in certain ways, or in categories, i.e. control rules, explanations, extra information rules that do not form part of the decision making function of the system. Selecting rules in isolation from the overall design usually distorts the knowledge unless it is extremely well formulated to begin with.

The process of mapping an expert's knowledge into a program's knowledge base is known as 'knowledge engineering'. This is not the elicitor's task unless the elicitor is also the knowledge engineer. We prefer to leave the explanation of knowledge representation to others. The magnitude and complexity of these issues make them beyond the scope of this book. We can, however, discuss how to model the knowledge so that it can readily be used as a method of intermediate representation.

5.4.5 Models of knowledge

Our task as knowledge elicitors is to create a model of the expert's domain, the knowledge, the reasoning or problem solving and not merely to extract data, rules or to represent the knowledge into some other machine representation (Kleer, De J., 1983; Lehtio, P., 1985). Our purpose is to provide a clear specification for the expert system by means of a conceptual model of expert system problem solving independently of implementation restraints.

Wielinga proposes that all implementation should be done from a complete knowledge model. Although in theory this can and probably should be done for completeness sake, we have found it is impossible to do in practice due to business demands. In practice we develop knowledge models from the transcripts, building an overall specification and continually model the knowledge while at the same time build the prototype in an incremental way.

Methods of creating a model

The role of the knowledge model is to help the elicitor grapple with the complexity and the sheer volume of the knowledge. The model reflects through separate characteristics and specific details, the object, task, plan or process, etc. Therefore there are several models, such as design models, knowledge models, task models, user models, communication between system and user models and so on. Each one is a description of the strategy of the expert (or the expert system) and the knowledge that is brought to bear to achieve a goal or function.

Our methods, are influenced by Knowledge Analysis Documentation Structuring (KADS). Wielinga states the KADS is a 'conceptual modelling language which can be used as an intermediary representation between data on expertise and the design/implementation of an expert system'. The theory is based on a view of expert problem-solving behaviour and it holds that 'it is possible and useful to distinguish between several generic types of knowledge . . . and that these types of knowledge can be organized in layers, which have limited interaction'.

Like Breuker and Wielinga we also describe the knowledge as

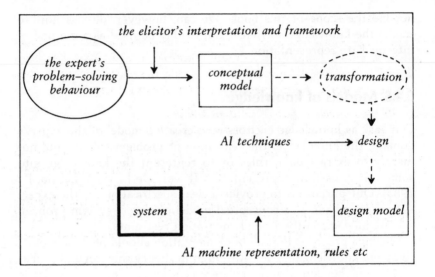

Figure 5.1   The KBS modelling development process

belonging to a layer. There is a task layer, the (inference layer) or rule layer, and the domain layer.

The task (layer) knowledge produces knowledge about the break-down of the tasks within each goal or sub-goal. Accordingly the knowledge is analysed to form a task hierarchy into which the control layer can be applied. This control layer shows how the tasks and sub-tasks are ordered according to the function of the proposed system, for example, a business function.

The inference or the rule layer is the explanation factor, knowledge that explains or puts forward a hypothesis to account for certain facts or reasons for the expert's behaviour. This knowledge is the organizing factor and is used for the design model, which can then be re-modelled into a detailed system design model and subse-quently into system code.

The rules should be categorized within each sub-task and within an overall task so that they can be easily organized in the knowledge base. Additionally the concept types upon which the rules are put into action must be identified and connections made to concepts in the domain layer. From these an inference plan may be built. The domain knowledge describes the concepts and elements in the domain and how one concept is related to another.

Rules in categories

There are many methods of machine implementation, these may include rules, frames etc. For our example, if a decision has been made to represent knowledge for a rule based system then conditional statements or rules are of the following form.

If: there is evidence that A and B are true
Then: conclude that there is evidence that C is true

Not long ago it was common practice literally to 'find' rules in the raw interview transcripts and implement them straight into machine code. This practice resulted in rules that were often misrepresentative of the knowledge. Additional elicitation then further assisted understanding of the knowledge, this had the effect of making rules obsolete or simply wrong, and new or revised rules had to be formulated instead.

The practice now is to understand the knowledge within a context and to understand the significance of the rules rather than placing them in unidentified lists. Rules should be placed in categories, so that a control structure can be easily implemented. The engineer can then organize the knowledge base, knowing where certain rules can be found. For example, under the category of occupation the following rule may apply. The rules will also be categorized under a function, or task, for example, the assessment of applicant for standard rating.

If: occupation has a significant manual element
And: applicant is otherwise acceptable at standard rates
Then: occupation may be suitable for a shorter deferred period

Further sub-categorization may be manual occupations, standard rates or shorter deferred period and (task) acceptable assessment of client for standard rating.

The definite form the rule takes here is at the knowledge level. The implementation formulation of the rule will be different depending on the method of implementation and the tools used.

Analysing the expert's task using task models

The expert's task can be modelled at several levels. High level expert tasks are used in reaching a goal, which we depict graphically. What form this takes is individualistic. One suggestion is to draw all the expert's tasks in the centre of a box or circle, all sources of information received by the expert in the performance of a task are outside the box, as are all other inputs and outputs to the task, which may include data inputs or outputs. The tasks within the box are then broken down individually and the process is repeated until all the sub-tasks have been extensively analyzed and exposed in this way. Rules and concepts can then be applied to each specific sub-task within the context of each task or goal.

This method of documentation can show which tasks are generic within a particular domain. These task structures can be used if the order of the tasks changes, for instance, if the expert wishes to apply another strategy.

The details of other formalisms, their relative merits and defects, are all covered extensively elsewhere, and is in any case beyond the intended range of this book. (See for instance: Brachman, R. and Levesque, J.)

5.5 INDIRECT METHODS AND PSYCHOMETRIC TECHNIQUES

We have emphasized the interview as a means of knowledge elicitation primarily because we believe it has not received the necessary amount of practical discussion that such a powerful and flexible tool deserves. This does not mean to say that we do not recognize the valuable contribution that other techniques have to offer.

The difference between the direct and indirect method of interviewing is: that in the direct method the expert is the only source of information, the elicitor relies in total on the expert's utterance in an interview, i.e. 'tell me what you know', whereas in the indirect method the elicitor is effectively saying 'let me test what I think you know'.

The use of an indirect method will aid the expert to supply knowledge that the expert may not normally be able to divulge in an interview. The expert may not be able to describe verbally the finer details of the knowledge used, whereas with the aid of, say, a repertory grid, the elicitor can draw out the details required (Boose, J., 1988.)

5.5.1 The techniques

There are several indirect techniques to choose from:

• Questionnaires

- Lists
- Tables
- Trees — hierarchies, vertical
- Networks — free association, clustering
- Physical space — description, drawing
- Physical model — path analysis

Questionnaires

Questionnaires might be categorized as a direct method of interviewing but here they are classed as indirect because they do not automatically constitute part of the routine elicitation interview. They are used only if the interview methods have failed to firmly establish required information or an important aspect of it. Questionnaires are useful for:

- discovering variables;
- open-ended questions before an intense structured interview;
- combining expertise from different expert sources;
- gaining a substantial amount of information from many sources in the domain, a large number of users say, in the shortest time;
- establishing and correcting uncertainties in variables or rules.

The questionnaires can be in various forms such as:

Question: Risk factor > .06 How certain are you of this risk factor?
Answer: Extremely certain / reasonably certain / borderline / reasonably uncertain / extremely uncertain.
or:
Uncertain _____ Certain
Put an x on the scale that indicates your response.
or:
Give a value from 0 = uncertain, to 100 = certain.

The questionnaire should not confine the expert's knowledge too narrowly. The expert should not have to explain too much, simple answers usually suffice. The elicitor must use judgement to decide what an appropriate answer would be, and how much detail is necessary, allowing space for more if necessary.

The wording of a question can easily change its meaning. At first glance two questions may seem similar, for example, if the elicitor were trying to find out about the kind of territory appropriate for military tanks, the elicitor might ask:

'On what terrain would you use tanks?'

The expert can then indicate what terrain is suitable for this particular weapon. If the elicitor had not thought carefully enough about the phrasing of the question, and had instead asked:

'Where would it be appropriate to use tanks?'

The elicitor would inadvertently be asking a much broader question despite the superficial similarity of form. It would be equally appropriate to mention many factors in addition to those concerning the terrain which would affect the use of tanks, for example, strategic information.

Producing a questionnaire for the expert, to elicit precisely the information that the elicitor needs, is more difficult than it might seem. The elicitor must think carefully about what kind of information is expected to be received when planning the questionnaire. There is nothing more irritating for the expert than finding a one-line space for an answer that would require a whole page, or finding that the elicitor has mis-managed the question. The elicitor should think about testing the effects that various types of questions draw from test respondents, and should be particularly vigilant for ambiguities in phrasing, restructuring questions whenever necessary.

Whatever the approach taken by the elicitor it is essential always to leave some space at the end of the questionnaire for any additions the respondents may wish to add. It may be that even though the questions were correct in the sense of assisting the elicitor to acquire the information sought, there may be more that the respondent wishes to add for the sake of clarity or completeness.

Lists

Lists of concepts are very useful for quick reference and can be extended into a data dictionary. These lists can constitute an important part of the documentation and reference.

Word lists in categories, separated by their similarity, difference, relation or some other categorization, also provide a quick and clear means of feedback. Presenting the expert with such lists, to check for completeness or accuracy, is a useful device for shortening the reviewing time before starting the next interview.

However the elicitor should be aware of some possible limitations of lists. For example:

• Listing words accordingly to their frequency of occurrence often results in bias, and can be seriously misleading unless understood within the more general framework of the domain.

- Some words and concepts will be too general to be meaningful without contextual information, and may be misleading if they have popular associations outside of the domain. More information than just a list of words is required to contextualize and qualify.
- The expert may have given an incomplete response, and lists alone may fail to elicit missing, unusual or complex information or connections.
- The elicitor must carefully record any limitations of generality and scope that apply. A concept without such information may later suggest, erroneously, that its scope is universal.

Concept sorting

When the major concepts have been isolated from the interview transcript, they are written on cards, each on a separate card, and given to the expert in a totally random order so that they can be sorted through and laid out in clusters showing relationships into which they naturally fall within the scope of the view of the domain. The cards test for hierarchical priorities ('parent/child' relationships), dependencies, similarities and differences and so on. Many variants on this basic method are used:

- The expert is given concepts and asked to say why or in what way two of them are alike and thereby different from the third.
- Alternatively many cards are spread out randomly in front of the expert, and two cards are selected which are alike, different, of the same family and so on.
- The test can be expanded further, questioning the expert on differences between the two, three or four cards, or by adding or subtracting a card, then asking the expert if the categories have been changed by the addition or removal of a card.
- The expert can arrange the cards in hierarchies, trees, in a decision-making ladder or in order of importance. The elicitor then questions the expert about the relationships, why one concept is placed higher than another or why it is grouped with another, and so on.

This technique is very simple to use and the number of concepts can be reduced or sub-divided to simplify the process further. But the elicitor must be aware that the very simplicity of the method can cause problems. While it is useful for eliciting information about dependencies, relationships and so forth, the elicitor must be aware of much wider issues such as the environmental context, users and so on. It is a useful assistant but a very bad master.

Repertory grid techniques

In 1955 a psychologist named George Kelly designed a technique for elucidating the way people constructed their mental schemes, and which he described as a method of 'going beyond words'. He called it Personal Construct Theory (Kelly, G., 1955). Detailed discussion and instructions of the technique and its application are well beyond the range of this book. The subject is well covered elsewhere however (Fransella F., 1977). We will confine the discussion to a brief survey.

Before the elicitor can design a grid, it is necessary to know about constructs and elements:

> a CONSTRUCT is something that can be qualitative or quantitative, ie, higher, better.

> ELEMENTS are names of things such as, the King of Hearts, Jack of all Trades.

The elements must be members of a class and be representative of their class. The elements of knowledge can either be elicited direct from the expert or supplied from textbooks.

Types of grids include, the rank order grid, the rating grid and the implications grid. Grids can be used to measure cognitive differentiation, intensity and complexity. They can also validate knowledge, expose meanings and provide accurate measurements.

Example

In a rank ordered grid, the elements; say types of cards for instance:

- *king of hearts*
- *queen of clubs*
- *jack of diamonds*
- *ten of spades*
- *eight of diamonds*
  etc.

These card types are written on the back of several small cards and numbered. The constructs become the most preferred suit, the highest numbered card, the most attractive picture card and so on. Supposing that the cards are being investigated for ranking order.

After the construct type and number are written on the front of the small cards, the expert rank orders the small cards by the criteria implicit in the construct type. In this way the ambiguity of the Ace, which may be the highest or lowest numbered card is uncovered.

Using repertory grid technique

The grid is used to identify limitations and boundaries between and among related ideas at the opposite ends of a spectrum. Concepts, such as 'like' and 'hate' are placed on opposite axis of a grid. There are several ways to elicit differences, the elicitor can ask the expert simply: 'these are two buildings, but can you tell me the ways they are alike and how they are different, or at what point do they become houses or cease to be mansions or cottages?'

When for example an expert has stated of some relationship, 'that looks all right to me', the expert's definition of what 'looks all right' can be tested by closer comparisons with other objects, which are judged specifically by what is correct and by the way they 'look'.

We have noted the fact that some experts are inarticulate, and that even among the more articulate ones, it is often difficult consciously to state what they do in practice all the time. The expert may have great difficulty in differentiating one concept and its meaning from another and even, if it is possible, he/she may have difficulty in telling the elicitor how it is difficult. This is the attraction of repertory grid technique. It is easy to see in the light of all these considerations why this technique, which relies on illustrative comparisons without needing to unpack the conceptual content, was adapted from the original use in psychology to become a tool in knowledge elicitation.

Sorting by dyads or triads or elements

Dyads and triads describe the number of elements that may be compared with each other. A simple example of a dyad compares, for example, a dog with a cat, a triad compares a boat, a ship and an ocean liner. The expert describes the differences and similarities of each element in relation to the construct. In this description, the expert describes the physical attributes or the use. The expert may not volunteer implicit information, for example, that merchant seamen refer to ships as boats.

By laddering

This method is used to elicit elements of higher abstraction. The elicitor, by a probing technique, metaphorically 'pushes' the expert up the rungs of the ladder, eliciting deeper meanings between the elements and their constructs, until the relevant information is abstracted.

Laddering can be used informally during normal interviews, or in a more formal situation. If used informally during an interview, insert questions such as 'Can you give me another example of X?' or 'What other incidences like X occur?'. The elicitor starts with a core object and tries to find out if there are any other instances within that particular context.

Used in a formal context, the questions are asked in isolation. For example, 'Can you think of all the objects that X has?' or 'What is the common factor of X?'. As these questions are asked out of context variations in the knowledge are difficult to spot and many of the elements elicited may be unnecessary and not used by the expert (and system) in the solution of a problem.

The elicitor's method of probing is important, and should be subtle. Sometimes asking the expert to repeat or rephrase answers that will elicit further abstractions and add to their distinctiveness. The context should always be taken into account as the elements may change accordingly.

Laddering can go down, up and sideways, depending on what hierarchies the elicitor is trying to develop.

Unidimensional and multidimensional scaling

There are a number of scaling techniques, and clustering of concepts by proximity.

Papers (Burton, A., 1987; Cooke, N., 1987; Young, R., 1987) extensively discusses psychometric methods of multidimensional scaling, ultra metric trees, additive trees, additive clustering and extended trees. In brief, the method of unidimensional scaling represents objects as points along a line. It is used for modelling objects that are suspected as being more important or relevant than another (dominance relations) and proximity relations among objects. If objects differ on more than one attribute then using more than one way of looking at them (multidimensional scaling) is more appropriate.

Multidimensional scaling can also be used for visual data, the differences of drawings or sketches may be indistinguishable to the elicitor or novice, but to the expert they are distinct.

Advantages

The great advantage of using the grid is that data from a single expert can be subjected to various statistically based methods of group analysis. The grid can be extremely useful for bringing to light and underlying structure of the expert's thinking, together with concepts that were previously not thought to have much importance, additional knowledge that was not known to have a relationship with another part and so on. The use of construct theory enables the elicitor to look at concepts in a narrower context, and in smaller numbers, which is often difficult to do in the larger context of the interview.

Problems to look out for

The danger with its use is that it may be used inappropriately by those without knowledge of the underlying assumptions of the original theory or elicitation methodology. The risk is indiscriminate use, applied in any and every situation, for all types of knowledge. Anyone using it should be aware of the underlying assumptions, and ensure that what they are testing really is what they intended. It becomes inefficient if the grid is used uncritically as an instrument, without due attention paid to the analysis and interpretation of the results.

1. A construct must always operate within a context.
An expert will use a concept in relation to a particular context and may use the same word, but with a different use in another context. This difference or sameness of each concept must be held within the appropriate context or environmental conditions.

2. There must be a limitation of concepts that the construct will produce.
The knowledge from a construct must be bound, i.e. the elicitor must have some idea of the limitations of the meanings of the concepts. Otherwise the list of concepts will get longer and wider, the differences more and more obscure, until the amount of information becomes uncontrollable and impossible to analyse and may not be requisite knowledge.

3. The meaning, and knowledge about, the concepts should be known.
The construct is not a method for eliciting new concepts, it is a

method of finding relationships, similarities and differences among known concepts, and validating the knowledge already found.

4. That the expert and elicitor agree the same 'meaning' of what is being measured.

The results of the process will be as good as the designer. There may be many ways that the constructs can be analysed and many inferences can be made about the information they contain. It is not true to say that the construct method is a more objective or scientific test of knowledge. It is still as wide open to bias, lack of thought, bad judgement, or bad design methodology as an interview could be. That the expert will respond to what is 'perceived', is the purpose of the test.

5. The concepts elicited should be bipolar, ie, by stating what a concept is, it is also implying what it isn't.

Uses

Methods for finding variables and attributes are:

- Multidimensional scaling
- Hierarchical clustering   Ordered trees
- Concept sorting

Methods for finding relationships are:

- Query for completeness
- Concept sorting

Method for organization:

- Concept sorting

5.5.5 Where and when to use these techniques?

There are two issues important to consider when using these techniques: 1. Where are such techniques most suitable? and 2. How does the elicitor judge when and where they should be used?

1. The use of a variety of indirect interviewing techniques may be preferable for several reasons:

- The time factor may be crucial. It may be convenient for the elicitor to present some well prepared tests for the expert to perform, either in their own time or with the elicitor present.

- The elicitor may need 'precision' knowledge for crucial decision making on behalf of the system.
- There may be a suitable indirect technique which will elicit certain kinds of knowledge but which another more direct technique may not.
- The expert may respond better to indirect interviewing techniques, and may even prefer them.
- For experimental purposes.

2. These methods are most useful:

- As a means of refining and quantifying knowledge, and perhaps, uncovering very subtle distinctions and gradations of meaning. This suggests that they are best used as an auxiliary tool,
- As a means of testing and checking what has already been revealed, rather than as a means for discovery.
- In the case of an inarticulate expert, here they would be essential,
- In knowledge areas where there are many subtle gradations to be considered, where the domain is largely numeric or very highly structured, or where time is short.

6 An overview of the methods

6.1 SUMMARY

The most important aspects of elicitation are recapitulated in this summary. Hopefully having read about the process in more depth, this summary will draw the whole process together, and give the practitioner a useful overview.

6.1.1 Characterizing the process

The elicitor's task is to understand an expert's skill. During this process the elicitor is likely to be faced with an ever increasing mass of heterogeneous information from the expert, and needs to find the keys to structure and organization within the expert's knowledge. However these keys are rarely apparent immediately: revealing them constitutes the major challenge of successful knowledge elicitation.

Without proper organization, the process of collecting information from the expert can too easily degenerate into confusion, one of the causes of frequent misunderstanding. The failure to distinguish what is relevant is the main cause of many problems such as the possibility of antagonism between expert and elicitor.

Lack of good organization can also cause psychological frustration: a lack of visible progress, inability to demonstrate what understanding (if any) has been achieved and the possibility that the documentation will be inadequate, reflecting this ambiguity and confusion. Worse, perhaps, is the almost inevitable demoralization, and consequent de-motivation of the expert that may follow, making all further elicitation sessions that much more difficult.

Clearly, then the first pre-requisite is a controlled and structured process of knowledge elicitation. This is achieved, by: (a) creating VIEWS of the domain, each of which represents a smaller area for the elicitor to concentrate attention. Unless the elicitor is dealing with a very small and simple domain, it is advisable to sub-divide; and (b) by LAYERING the information. That is, using iteration, to move downwards from general high level characteristics, through successive levels of greater and greater detail until the required level of detail has been achieved (often referred to as the knowledge granularity), for a particular project.

Creating the VIEWS

Although it is always possible for practitioners to develop their own basic domain view categories, we suggest the flexible application of five basic views:

1. characteristics of the expert
2. matters relating to the domain knowledge
3. the domain environment
4. the users in the domain
5. the project requirements

These are applied where relevant and can be adapted and changed to exploit any naturally occurring structural possibilities within a specific knowledge domain. Chapter 2 is devoted to this issue of structuring the elicitation process.

LAYERING the knowledge

The process of elicitation is also controlled by layering the knowledge. Within any view, or even within the domain as a whole, the elicitor begins to acquire high level information and proceeds in a cyclic fashion to probe further and deeper into the detail of the expert's skill within that specific area.

Each step is planned carefully in advance in consultation with the expert and the elicitation process is carried out in a series of iterative passes, each pre-set at a specific level of detail and focused on an pre-arranged area. These plans are continually reviewed (in consultation with the expert), as the process unfolds. There must be some flexibility in time-tabling interviews since progress in a linear fashion and at a constant rate is seldom achieved.

Types of interview

The interviewing cycle is further structured by applying different interview techniques at different stages of the process:

- The first phase, which might require several sessions, involves OUTLINE interviewing, where the elicitor seeks more general high level information by allowing the expert to provide an overview of the area in question.
- The middle phase uses the STRUCTURED interview technique, to acquire increasingly detailed information, and the elicitor probes for submerged aspects of the knowledge.
- When the elicitor is more confident and has a better grasp of the domain and the expertise, interviewing techniques which emphasize discovering strategies, testing and validation of the knowledge model are required, such as the THINK ALOUD technique, where the expert describes solving a problem while thinking aloud.
- The elicitor has a choice of using various other tools where the need arises, for example: indirect, or techniques such as card sorting or repertory grid.

Analysis of transcripts

Once the elicitor has got the raw information from the expert, it must be subjected to detailed analysis and scrutiny. Using such techniques as Conceptual Analysis and Task Analysis the elicitor can begin to build a profile of the material, constructing concept and data dictionaries, making charts and diagrams of the task and problem-solving behaviour. Ultimately the elicitor attempts to build a representation of the expert's knowledge for system building, training or archiving.

Planning

We stress the need for careful planning. Planning must also include agreement on company strategies and corporate decisions, manager's support, realistic budgets and human time scales, which all require thought and realistic assessment if any project is to succeed.

The planning we refer to here is solely concerned with knowledge elicitation:

- Plan the content and direction of the interviews, and be meticulous when preparing equipment and materials. *Before* the process starts.
- Every stage should be planned in advance and agreed and time-

tabled with the expert. This planning should be continually monitored by the elicitor, so that any changes or deviations can be accommodated and understood as soon as possible, and their effects allowed for.

• Each actual interview should be preceded by a review of progress for the expert to check, correct and agree the analysis of work done so far and to review and revise plans in the light of actual progress.

This elicitation process is a top down, breadth first, iterative sequence of interviews with the expert, where agreed, controlled layers of knowledge emerge, enabling the elicitor to construct an incrementally developed picture of the expertise.

Preparation

What follows is a checklist of preparatory considerations. It is not exhaustive, there may be many other things, often arising out of the particular context in which the elicitor works, which can be added to the list. We suggest a three-part approach: (1) preparation of the expert; (2) preparation of the environment; (3) preparation of the equipment.

Preparing the expert

This is the most important part of preparation.

• Try to contact the expert beforehand and discuss any preparatory requirements.

• It is usually worth spending a little time explaining the process in outline, and introducing the various methods of interviewing that you will use and what they are supposed to achieve. The expert then has the opportunity to raise informally any questions or problems that may be foreseen and provisional planning and timetabling can begin.

• Think about the motivation of the expert. Can anything be done to reassure any concern about the role as expert, or try to ensure enthusiasm about what lies ahead?

How does the expert feel about the whole process of elicitation? How well motivated is the expert towards participating in what might appear a difficult, even intimidating, process. Since you as the elicitor will be spending a great deal of time with the expert, it is well worth considering the informal aspects of your working relationship. What does the expert REALLY feel about the process? Can the elicitor give any information or reassurance that will make things easier?

It is not unusual for people to feel that they are losing control of their expertise, an intimate part of themselves in effect, by undergoing knowledge elicitation. They do not usually know what will be expected of them, or about simple but important practical matters such as how long the process will take. All the things can be discussed informally before the start and contribute to the smooth running of the formal elicitation process.

The above considerations are more important, not less, if the expert is unfamiliar with computers and computer based tools. If you are planning to use indirect elicitation techniques, such as questionnaires or scaling techniques, does the expert understand what will be required of him or her.

If a machine based elicitation technique is used, it is essential to consider how much previous exposure the expert has had to computers and computer software. How does the expert feel about their use? Would some introductory sessions be useful? It is certainly foolhardly to avoid the personal and human dimension of knowledge elicitation. Time spent by the elicitor acquiring and developing personal skills is seldom wasted (and may pay dividends in other contexts). Though there can be no substitute for personal experience, courses and literature on communication skills are becoming more widely available (Davies, M and Hakiel, S., 1988).

Preparation can be done quickly and efficiently with forethought, and could make a substantial difference to all that follows. Make this integral to the elicitation process. Include time for preparation in any planning estimates. Preparation is essential rather than just useful and needs to be thought through very early in the process development cycle.

Preparing the environment

The optional environment for knowledge elicitation will be determined by an individual elicitation context and is often, therefore, a matter of using common sense and exploitation of local opportunities. However, there are still some general considerations to review in advance.

- Bear in mind the general dynamics of interviewing: plan the seating arrangements to enhance comfort rather than formality.
- Have the participants sit in a circle or at the corners of tables; this

tends to be less formal and intimidating than sitting on opposite sides of a table.

- How do the participants feel about smoking?
- Can interruptions be controlled, or better still, prevented?
- Have reasonable breaks been provided for? Have coffee or tea been ordered?

It is useful to pay attention to detail. Every small effort contributes towards the impression of competence and efficiency which will help to relax and reassure the expert.

Equipment

Always ensure that:

- Equipment to be used in the interview is ready and works properly: recorders, props for simulations and so on.
- Take backup equipment (ideally standby recorder) and rehearse a changeover at least once so that you know what to do. Always have spare tapes and fresh batteries available.
- Notebooks, pens, pencils and the like should always be available, together with any models, diagrams, tools or manuals required.
- Ensure also that you have discussed with the expert any requirements for tools, models, diagrams or documents to illustrate and assist the explanation of expertise. Ascertain, if possible, not only what will be necessary but when it will be required and then ensure that it is there.

This may seem all too obvious, yet it is amazing how valuable elicitation time is lost for lack of the simplest things. A busy environment and pressing deadlines can easily obscure the obvious, so set aside five minutes well before the start of any session to check these things are covered.

The main elicitation cycle: a three phased approach

The basic pattern of the main elicitation process is: (A) Elicitation Phase; (B) Analysis Phase; (C) Review Phase.

The elicitation phase

Overview of Interviewing Techniques
We begin by interviewing the expert, using one of the appropriate interviewing techniques: (a) Outline Interviewing – for a general,

high level conceptual view and description of the domain (or some component view of it); (b) Structured Interviewing – for more depth of detail and the chance to probe the expert for possibly hidden conceptual and procedural knowledge; (c) Think Aloud Interviewing – where the expert talks as if a typical problem is attempted (or one of the indirect or psychometric techniques for confirmation and validation of what has been learned so far).

Note: In the think aloud interview the expert is asked to solve a specific problem, speaking some thoughts as the expert works through it. This procedure is similar to the post walk-through, an interview in which the expert is asked to remember a problem that has been solved already. The think aloud interview is therefore a more realistic account of the expert's actual behaviour and thoughts during a problem-solving session. The post walk-through is based on what the expert remembers of what was done, with less emphasis on what the thought processes were at the time. Therefore rationalization after the event is a much greater danger, the expert is more likely to tell the elicitor how the problem should have been solved, not what was actually done (Fox, J., 1980).

In general, judging when to change from one form of interview technique to the next is part of the elicitor's skill. This can only really be learned in practice.

The OUTLINE interview
To begin with, we wish to remain at a general, relatively superficial, conceptual level to get an overview of the whole domain or a particular part of it.

- Give the expert fairly general questions relating to each of the domain views, and let the answer be expressed freely and at length.
- This information should, when analysed, direct the elicitor's attention to the key areas, concepts and strategies where more in depth interviewing will be focused.
- It should also assist in identifying potential sources of difficulty, information which can then be fed back into further planning.

The elicitor is particularly (though not exclusively) interested in the expert's conceptual knowledge, wishing to get a feeling for what concepts and facts the expert will have to hand whenever the task is performed, though not yet needing to understand them or their implications in detail.

This OUTLINE interviewing technique is best used to orientate the elicitor and allow him or her to get a feeling for the domain and the expert's role within it to be gained. It may also be used for the feasibility study, as well as the opening orientation interviews for the main elicitation, and is particularly useful during the first pass over the whole domain to establish what domain VIEWS would be most useful.

The STRUCTURED interview

In subsequent interviews, we uncover the real depth and detail of the expert's knowledge, using the STRUCTURED interview. This will reveal the complexities of both the conceptual and strategic knowledge in each of the domain views. The elicitor plies the expert with more fine tuned and probing questions, some of which the elicitor will have devised from the previous analysis of the OUTLINE interviews, while others might occur out of immediate feedback from the answers that the expert gives.

The elicitor:

- attempts to set the level of detail at which the elicitor wants to question the expert, and tries (flexibly) to stick to that level,
- takes greater control of the interview than before, directing the expert to areas and aspects that are particularly of concern (though still allowing the expert to do the talking),
- probes the expert over points that seem to indicate deeper levels of knowledge than the higher level description seemed to indicate at first,
- carefully thinks about and formulates the questions so that the expert's answer will contain the right amount of information.

THINK ALOUD interview

Here, the expert is given a typical task or problem and is asked to comment aloud on the thinking and actions while attempting to solve the problem. This method is used to clarify and validate the knowledge gained so far. The elicitor should now have a more detailed understanding of the domain and the expert's role within it. So now it is far more likely that the elicitor will be able to follow the expert's behaviour when completing a task, or solving a problem.

The elicitor should be looking for evidence which seems to confirm or contradict the model of expert behaviour built in the previous interviewing sessions. It may be that the model can finally be established by watching the expert in action. Much useful control information may become apparent only when the expert is actually working on a problem, such as the order in which the sub-components are tackled, the knowledge required at different stages, and the 'where' and 'when' of different procedures applied in practice.

Thinking aloud while trying to solve a problem is often quite difficult for the expert at first. It is like holding a conversation while reading a book – try it and see how it feels. Apart from a few people who seem to have a natural ability to carry out several activities at the same time most of us find it difficult, and this is where help and consideration from the elicitor will be at a premium.

The analysis phase

The elicitor must then analyse the information after each interview. From the mass of verbal data provided by the expert in the interview, the elicitor attempts to construct a coherent pattern of behaviour, which can be reliably repeated by a knowledge based system to achieve the same result.

The major concepts are highlighted and documented, any information on the methods or procedures the expert uses must be similarly recorded. Any further questions, apparent gaps in the knowledge, for instance, or problems must be noted for further discussion and clarification with the expert. It is useful to develop a compressed version of what has been discovered so far, both as documentation of the work in progress and something to show the expert for checking and verification. By building interim representations, from each interview, of the facts, concepts and procedures, and by carefully analysing their interactions, relationships and dependencies, the elicitor can, incrementally, begin to reveal the structure of the expert's knowledge, which can then be used, maintained and updated as necessary.

The review phase

After a particular interview transcript (or notes, recording) has been analysed, we briefly review the result with the expert at the beginning of the next session. During this brief session the elicitor can:

• deal with any problems, or further questions,
• fill in gaps in the knowledge,
• clarify any obscure or difficult aspects.

This must obviously be done in a disciplined fashion to ensure it does not take up more than, say, the first ten minutes of the new interview. Should it appear that it will take more time, either change the topic of the current interview – if the expert agrees that the timetable allows – or arrange an additional clarification interview later.

This brief review serves to keep the whole elicitation process on course, allows a limited amount of problem-solving and validation to be done close to the context where the original knowledge was being discussed, and provides immediate feedback for the elicitor on the success of the effort, and for the expert on what has been achieved so far.

The time spent on review should be tightly controlled. It is not unusual to need more time than has been allowed originally, replanning is often necessary therefore flexible time budgets should be incorporated as part of the process. To call this time flexibility 'contingency' is misleading. Allocating contingency time implies that there is a reliable estimate of the time the elicitation will take and the additional time is for unforeseen but low probability events. Whereas the probability of the unforeseen in elicitation is high, because of the opaque and frequently submerged character of knowledge. Time allocations have to be continually checked and revised. This allows for both the possibility of exceptionally good progress where time is saved, and for unforeseen problems holding things up.

At the end it is advisable to try to clear up any small omissions, make any additions and deal with any clarifications or mistakes that have emerged. The review sessions at each interview should have reduced the amount of clearing up, but it is often worth allowing a final recapitulation session, to ensure that all ends are tied up, as a final validation of the elicitation process.

APPENDIX 1
The feasibility study

The feasibility study is like the full process of elicitation in miniature. It can therefore serve both to determine the viability of the project and, should it prove viable, constitute the first top level pass over the knowledge domain. It can provide information on:

- How best to sub-divide the domain and whether any modifications, extensions or additional divisions should be considered.
- Planning the following elicitation and helping to anticipate future needs and problems.
- How best to solve, or mediate any cultural, managerial or user resistance of the technology.

The only reason that the feasibility study is considered separately from the elicitation process is the special nature of its goal – whether or not further work is justified and what problems are likely to be encountered. The conventional feasibility study, incorporating business requirements, can therefore be carried out separately or later as part of the elicitation process.

The suitability criterion is determined by the expertise and knowledge domain. If the goal is an expert system it must be determined in advance that the expert's knowledge can be captured. The other issues such as cost, availability of resources, or the functionality of the end system are not considered here, not because they are not important but because they are discussed fully elsewhere (Barrett, M. and Beerel, A., 1988).

As in any other project area, failure to carry out the feasibility study makes any project very risky, and time, money and resources might be squandered needlessly. In addition a benefit is lost: the feasibility study can fill the role of a first pass, or overview, which feeds back information vital to the preparation of the rest of the elicitation process. Thus less interviewing time will be required in the first phase of the project, and the elicitor will already be familiar with the domain in outline.

The scope and duration of the feasibility study will obviously depend on particular contexts, and on factors like:

- availability of resources
- degree of doubt about technical feasibility
- the amount of experience both in knowledge elicitation techniques, and expert system building (if applicable)
- whether the knowledge or task is found to be suitable for expert system technology
- the particular organizational and contractual issues and factors.

The last factor has great importance and cannot be commented on in detail within this book. A more comprehensive discussion of organizational and contractual issues are given in other books although questions relating to these issues are included here. As a guideline for an average size project a properly conducted feasibility study of four or seven knowledge elicitation interviews (or less depending on the complexities of the task and domain), which last between one and two hours, will produce substantial amounts of knowledge and a grasp of the domain.

These questions are not inclusive but should give the reader some feel for the sort of answer that will help decide the question of feasibility. If, for instance, the task involves a large degree of subjective thought and does not involve overt behaviour from the expert, then difficulties may be unsurmountable. A certain amount of common sense is needed when applying these questions and analysing the answers, and also on the dependencies on a variety of factors arising from a given context. The information gained from these interviews should assist the developers to decide whether to continue with elicitation. It should reveal information about:

- the expert's task and function
- the nature of the knowledge
- the environment
- the language used by the expert
- the needs of the user
- any problems or special requirements in a particular case
- the intended role of the system

INFORMATION FROM THE FEASIBILITY STUDY

The following questions should reveal the type of information required at the feasibility stage and may also serve as a checklist for quick reference, especially helpful for beginners to knowledge elicitation.

A.1 Concerning the expert

(a) General

Questions

What is the role of the expert within the organization?
Does the expert fulfill a particular function?
What is the nature of the expert's speciality/field/knowledge?
Is the expert articulate? Available? Cooperative?
How long will the expert be required for elicitation, or how long is
    the expert willing to contribute knowledge?
Is the expert well motivated? Can there be further motivation?

Potential difficulties

The role of the expert may be central to a number of different tasks
    which may make extraction in a sub-context, or reorganization of
    the task structure difficult.
The expert's function may be unsuitable in principle for a system, eg.
    nursing.
The expert's field may be too highly specialized, or the knowledge
    may only be needed in highly specialized circumstances.
There may be problems gaining access to a busy expert.
Experts may not agree, might prove unsympathetic or uncooper-
    ative.
The expert may leave before the project is finished, or lose interest.

(b) The expert's function

Questions

What function does the expert fulfil?

How does the execution of the expert's role affect those who consult, i.e. the users.

What implications does this have for a potential system?

How much of the expert's role and function is it necessary to elicit information on?

Is it the whole of the expert's function, or particular tasks, or problem-solving behaviour?

How would any potential system assist the expert in the execution of the overall function?

(c) The expert's task/problem

Questions

What tasks must the expert carry out or what problems must be solved in order to fulfil the role?

Does the elicitation process need to capture the whole of the expert's overall task or just some of the sub-tasks or sub-problems?

Is each task discrete, or is one task closely connected with another?

Can the overall task or problem be decomposed into smaller units?

If it can, are these components homogeneous or heterogeneous?

Do the tasks involve moving from place to place?

Does the expert use references, or a manual?

A.2 Overview of the knowledge

(a) General

Questions

What is the structure, type and nature of the knowledge?

What is the overall function: problem-solving, diagnosis etc.?

Are there different levels (how 'deep' are the levels)?

What are the difficulties: extraction, complexity, or technical difficulties?

What type(s) of knowledge (heuristic, algorithmic)?

What are the constraints (environmental, personnel, etc.)?

Is the knowledge extensive?

Does the environment affect the knowledge to a large or small degree?

Problems

Some types of knowledge are unsuitable for a knowledge based system, i.e. mathematical or 'algorithmic' knowledge, because a conventional system would be better and simpler (although these kinds may be incorporated).

Some developers buy hardware and developmental environments before they understand the nature of their expert's knowledge and may be forced to distort it for representation purposes. Feasibility studies or some elicitation should be completed preferably before the purchase of machines.

Some domains are extremely technical and the language or jargon of the expert has to be learned before the expert feels able to communicate on a natural basis. Obviously learning difficult or technical terminology will take more time than a domain which is familiar to most people and this has to be taken account of in a project's time estimations.

Some environments will act as a physical constraint to elicitation.

Using a computer system might cause problems, or because of the complexity of the expertise a machine solution might alter the expert's or user's working environment detrimentally.

(b) Knowledge of decisions and problem-solving strategies

Questions

What kinds of strategies are used to carry out (i) the main task?
    (ii) any sub-tasks or procedures?
What kinds of difficulties does the expert experience when problem solving? Could a program cope with them?
Are there any symptoms of heuristic strategies? Or is it more likely that some strategies or procedures could be expressed algorithmically or by some other method?

Problems

The expert might need information from several 'outside' sources in order to make a decision.

A.3 Environment

Questions

What role does the expert's environment play (if any)?
If it is important, is it: central, or peripheral, or incidental?

Problems

The environment might impose particular constraints on the eventual systems' use or an elicitation, for example, an oil rig in the North Sea where factors such as weather, danger and so on could come into play.

A.4 The users

Questions

How do those who currently consult the expert perceive their requirements of an expert system? (for support, for making, or aiding decisions?)
Would this change significantly if they consulted a knowledge based system?
How do they feel about this?
Does the environment affect users differently?
Is there extensive user knowledge?
Has the user a special task/function as well as the expert?
Would they co-exist in a system easily?

Problems

The users may diverge from one another in their needs, training, knowledge, view of the domain or technical language.

A.5 General requirements and problems

(a) Time

Questions

What is the predicted total knowledge elicitation/engineering time?
What is the development time?

Can you identify the type of testing required?

Problems

Testing can be a lengthy and expensive process.
What happens if the project falls behind?
Can you have a contingency plan?

(b) Potential problem areas

Questions

Are there any potential difficulties with:
• the expert's methodology?
• ideas and theories the expert uses?
• those who will use the system?
• the expert's function?
• the extent or complexity of the knowledge?
• the environment in which the expert, or others affected by the
  project, work?
• any other more general constraints?

Problems

What if the methods or theories used within a domain are different?
What about variant interpretations of the domain knowledge by
  individual experts, or users?

(c) Developing a project plan

Questions

Are the requirements of all those involved consistent and explicit?
How many people need to be involved? Are they available when
  needed?
Is essential knowledge held by individuals or groups?
Are there machine needs that require extra attention or planning?
Is there a delivery plan?
How large are the costs? What about (machine availability) con-
  tingency plans?
How great are the benefits? Have they been explicitly evaluated?

Problems

The knowledge may be too involved or too voluminous to justify a
cost-effective system.
The resistance to a machine based system may be too strong, time
spent attempting to overcome this may be a necessary pre-
requisite.
The user benefits may be too small.
The machine requirements cannot be met.
The costs may be too high.
If the skills of the system building group are insufficient then it
might be more feasible to plan a project after these difficulties are
solved.

(d) The elicitation process itself

Questions

How much time is required for the knowledge elicitation interviews,
whether for the whole system or subsequent part of the
knowledge elicitation interviews?
What are the 'types' of knowledge used?

Problems

The expert or elicitor may not be able to give full-time commitment
to the project.
Other work or projects will make orientation more difficult for the
elicitor.

There is little point in attempting to provide more detailed assistance
for the feasibility study since each domain has to be assessed in the
light of the particular context in which the elicitor is working.
Nevertheless using the above guidelines and some commonsense it
should emerge quite quickly whether or not the project is feasible
from a technical point of view.

References

Adelson, B. (1984) 'When novices surpass experts: The difficulty of a task may increase with expertise'. *Journal of Experimental Psychology: Learning, Memory and Cognition*, vol. 10, pp. 483–95.

Anderson, J. (ed.) (1981). *Cognitive Skills and Their Acquisition*. Hillsdale, NJ: Laurence Erlbaum Associates.

Anderson, R. and Bower, G. (1983). *Human Associative Memory*. Washington, DC: Winston.

Aristotle. *The Categories. On Interpretation. Prior Analytics, Posterior Analytics Topica*. Loeb Classical Library, Cambridge, MA: Harvard University Press.

Bainbridge, L. (1986) 'Asking questions and assessing knowledge'. *Future Computing Systems*, vol. 1, no. 2.

Barrett, M. and Beerel, A. (1988). *Expert Systems in Business: A Practical Approach*. Englewood Cliffs, New Jersey: Ellis Horwood, Ltd.

Barthol, R. and Ku, N. (1980) 'Thinking aloud during reading'. *Scandinavian Journal of Psychology*, vol. 21, pp. 123–32.

Belnap, N. D., Steel, T. B., (1976) *The Logic of Questions and Answers*. New Haven: Yale University Press.

Belson, W. (1967) 'Tape-recordings: Its effects on accuracy of response in survey interviews'. *Journal of Marketing Research*, vol. 4, pp. 252–60.

Berry, D. C. and Broadbent, D. E. (1984) 'On the Relationship between Task Performance and Associated Verbalised Knowledge'. *Quarterly Journal of Experimental Psychology*, vol. 36A, pp. 209–31.

Berry, D. C. (1987) 'The problem with implicit knowledge'. *Expert Systems*, August 1987, vol. 4, no. 3.

Boose, J. H. (1985) 'A knowledge acquisition program for expert system based on personal construct psychology'. *International Journal of Man Machine Studies*, vol. 23, pp. 495–525.

Boose, J. H. (1986) 'Rapid acquisition and combination of knowledge from multiple experts in the same domain'. *Future Computing Systems*, vol. 1 (2), pp. 191–216.

Boose, J. H. (1988) A research framework for knowledge acquisition techniques and tools, in *Proceedings of the European Knowledge Acquisition Workshop* (EKAW '88). (eds) J. M. Boose, B. R. Gaines and M. Lunster, Sankt Augustin, West Germany, GMD, pp. 10.1–1.13.

174

Bouchon, B. and Yager, R. R. (eds) (1986). Uncertainty in Knowledge Based Systems. International Conference on Information Processing and Management of Uncertainty in Knowledge Based Systems. Paris, France, June/July, 1986. Publ. Springer-Verlag.

Bobrow, E. and Collins, A. (1975) 'Reasoning from Incomplete Knowledge'. In *Representation and Understanding. Studies in Cognitive Psychology*, (eds A. Collins *et al.*). New York: Academic Press Incl. pp. 103-29.

Brachman, Ronald J. and Levesque, Hector, J. (eds) *Readings in Knowledge Representation*, Los Altos, California: Morgan Kaufman Publishers Inc.

Breuker, J. L. and Wielinga, B. J. (1987) 'Use of models in the interpretation of verbal data'. In *Knowledge Acquisition for Expert Systems: A Practical Handbook* (ed. A. L. Kidd). New York: Plenum Press, pp. 17-44.

Breuker, J. A. and Wielinga, B. J. (1987) 'Knowledge acquisition as modelling expertise: The KADS methodology'. Proceedings of the First European Workshop on Knowledge Acquisition for Knowledge-Based Systems, Reading, UK, 2-3 September, 1987, Reading: Reading University, section B1.

Breuker, J. A. et al. (1987). 'Model-driven knowledge acquisition interpretation models' Deliverable task AI, Esprit Project 1098, Amsterdam: University of Amsterdam.

Broadbent, D. (1971) *Decision and Stress*. London: Academic Press.

Buchanan, B. and Feigenbaum, E. (1978) 'DENDRAL and Meta-DENDRAL. Their applications dimension'. *Artificial Intelligence*, vol. 11, pp.5-24.

Burton, A. M. and Shadbolt, N. R. (1987b) 'A formal evaluation of knowledge elicitation techniques for expert systems: domain 1' in *Knowledge Acquisition for Engineering Applications*, (eds) C. J. Pavelin and M. D. Wilson pp. 20-8.

Buscher, R. Fritz, C. and Quarantelli, E. (1956) 'Tape-recorded interviews in social research.' *American Social Review*. vol. 21, no. 3, pp. 359-64.

Carnegie, Dale (1981) *How to Gain Friends and Influence People*. London: Octopus Press.

Chandrasekaran, B. (1987) 'Towards a functional architecture for intelligence based on generic information processing tasks'. Proceedings of the 10th International Joint Conference on AI (IJCA1-87) Milan, Italy 23-8 August 1987.

Chase, W. G. and Simon, H. A. (1973) 'Skill and Working Memory', in *The Psychology of Learning and Motivation*, (ed. G. H. Bower) vol. 16, New York: Academic Press.

Clancey, W. (1983) 'The epistomology of a rule based expert system: A framework for explanation', *Artificial Intelligence*, vol. 20, pp. 215-51.

Clancey, W. J. (1986) 'Heuristic Classification' in *Knowledge Based Problem Solving*, Englewood Cliffs. N. J.: Prentice Hall, pp. 1-67.

Cooke, N. M. and McDonald, J. E. (1987). 'The application of psychological scaling techniques to knowledge elicitation for knowledge-based systems'. *International Journal of Man-Machine Studies*, vol. 26, pp. 533-50.

Crispin, L. Hamilton, W. and Trickey, G. (1984) 'The relevance of visual sequential memory to reading'. *British Journal of Educational Psychology*, vol. 54, pp. 24-30.

Davies, M. and Hakiel, S. (1988) 'Knowledge harvesting', a practical guide to interviewing. *Expert System* vol. 5, pp. 42-50.

Dretske, F. (1983) 'The précis of knowledge and the flow of information'. *The*

Behavioural and Brain Sciences, vol. 6 pp. 55–90. Cambridge University Press, Cambridge.

Downes, C., Smeyak, G. and Martin, E. (1980) *Professional Interviewing*, New York: Harper & Row Publishers.

Duncan, S. and Fiske, D. W. (1977) *Face to Face Interaction*. New Jersey, Erlbaum, Hillsdale.

Easterby-Smith, M. (1981) 'The design and analysis and interpretation of repertory grids', in *Recent Advances in Personal Construct Psychology*. (ed. M. L. G. Shaw), London: Academic Press, pp. 9–30.

Eden, C. and Jones, S. (1984) 'Using repertory grids for problem construction'. *Journal of the Operational Research Society*, vol. 35 (a), pp. 779–90.

Evans, J. St., (1988) 'The knowledge elicitation problem: a psychological perspective.' *Behaviour and Information Technology*, vol. 7, no. 2, pp. 111–30.

Feigenbaum, E. and McCorduck, P. (1984) *The Fifth Generation*, London: Pan Books.

Fox, J. (1980) 'Making decisions under the influence of memory.' *Psychological Review*, vol. 87, no. 2, pp. 190–211.

Fox, J. (1984) 'Doubts about induction', SPL — *Insight bulletin*, vol. 2 (2), pp. 31–6.

Fransella, F., Bannister, D. (1977) *A Manual for Repertory Grid Technique*, London: Academic Press.

Frenkel-Brunswick, E. (1949) 'Intolerance of ambiguity as an emotional variable', *Journal of Personality*, vol. 18, pp. 108–43.

Gaines, B. and Boose, J. (1988) *Knowledge Acquisition for Knowledge Based Systems*, vol. 1, London: Academic Press.

Guildford, J. (1967) *The Nature of Human Intelligence*. Maidenhead: McGraw-Hill.

Hart, A. (1988) *Expert Systems for Managers*, London: Kogan Page.

Hayes-Roth, F. Waterman, D. A. and Lenat, D. B. (eds) (1983) *Building Expert Systems*, Reading, MA: Addison Wesley.

Hayes-Roth, B. and Walker, C. (1979) 'Configural effects in human memory.' *Cognitive Sciences*.

Hayward, S. A., Wielinga, B. and Breuker, J. (1987) 'Structured analysis of knowledge', *International Journal of Man-Machine Studies*, vol. 26, pp. 487–98.

Henderson, J. and Nutt, P. (1980) 'The influence of decision style on decision-making behaviour', *Management Science*, vol. 26, no. 4.

Kahneman, D. and Tversky, A. (1972) 'Subjective probability. A judgement of representatives', *Cognitive Psychology*. vol. 3, pp. 430–54.

Kelly, G. (1955) *The Psychology of Personal Constructs* (two volumes), New York, NY: W. W. Norton.

Kleer, De J. and Seely-Brown, J. (1983) 'Assumptions and ambiguities in mechanistic mental models.' In *Mental Models*, (eds) Gentner, D. and Stevens, A. New Jersey: Laurence Erlbaum Associates.

Kolodner, J. (1983) 'Towards an understanding of the role of experience in the evolution from novice to expert. In *Developments in Expert Systems*, (ed) M. J. Coombs, London: Academic Press, pp. 95–116.

Kounin, J. S. (1941) 'Experimental studies of rigidity'. *Character and Personality*, vol. 9, pp. 251–82.

Lehnert, W. G. (1978) *The Process of Question-answering*. Hillsdale N.Y.: Laurence Erlbaum Associates.

Lehtio, P. (1985) 'Verifying autobiolographical facts' *Cognition*, vol. 26, pp. 39–58.

Lenat, D. (1982) 'The nature of heuristics' *Artificial Intelligence*, vol. 19, no. 2, pp. 189–249.

Lenat, D. (1983) 'The role of heuristics in learning by discovery: Three case studies'. In *Machine Learning: An Artificial Intelligence Approach*, (eds) R. Michalski, J. Carbonell and T. Mitchell, Palo Alto, California: Tioga Publishing Co.

Lyle, Jane (1989) *Understanding Body Language*, Mandarin, Hong Kong: Hamlyn.

Marcus, S. and M. McDermott (1989) 'SALT: A knowledge acquisition language for propose and revise systems'. *Artificial Intelligence*, vol. 39, pp. 1–37.

McCarthy, J. (1958) 'Programs with common sense'. In *Proceedings of the Symposium on the Mechanisation of Thought Processes*, pp. 77–84. Cambridge, MA: MIT Press, 1968. (Reprinted in *Semantic Information Processing*, ed. M. Minsky, 109–18.

Michalski, R. S. V. and Chilansky, R. L. (1980) 'Knowledge acquisition by encoding expert rules versus computer induction from examples: a case study involving soybean pathology'. *International Journal of Man Machine Studies*, vol. 12 (1), pp. 63–87.

Mickalski, R. S. and Stepp, R. E. (1983) 'Learning from observation: conceptual clustering'. In *Machine Learning: An Artificial Intelligence Approach* (eds) R. Mikalski, J. Carbonell, and T. Mitchell, Palo Alto, California: Tioga Publishing Co., pp. 331–63.

Miller, G. (1956) 'The magical number 7, plus or minus 2, some limits on our capacity for processing information'. *Psychological Review*, vol. 63, pp. 81–97.

Miller, G. (1978) 'The psychology of communication. Seven essays, *Psychological Review*, vol. 63, pp. 81–97.

Mitchell, Colin (1989) 'Expert systems: A management opportunity'. In *Expert Systems '89. Applications and methods in Knowledge-Based Systems*. The British Computer Society.

Mittal, S. and Dym, C. L. (1985) 'Knowledge acquisition from multiple experts'. *AI Magazine*, vol. 5 (2), pp. 32–6.

Morik, K. (1987) Knowledge acquisition and machine learning, the issue of modelling. Proceedings of the first European Workshop on Knowledge Acquisition for Knowledge Based Systems. Reading UK. 2–3 September 1987, Reading. Reading University, Section A 4.

Murphy, G. L. and Wright, J. C. (1984) 'Changes in conceptual structure with expertise: Differences between real world experts and novices'. *Journal of Experimental Psychology: Learning, Memory and Cognition*, vol. 10, pp. 144–55.

Nii, H. P. (1983) Quoted in Feigenbaum and P. McCorduck. *The Fifth Generation*. London. Pan Books, pp. 80–4.

Nisbett, R. and Ross, L. (1974) 'Psychodynamics versus psychologic'. Human Influences. In *Judgement under Uncertainty. Heuristics and Biases*. (eds) D. Kahnaman, P. Slovic and A. Tversky. Cambridge: Cambridge University Press.

Payne, S. L. (1951) *The Art of Asking Questions*. New Jersey: Princetown University Press.

Pease, Alan (1981) *Body Language: How to Read Others' Thoughts by Their Gestures*. London: Sheldon Press.

Rees, E. (1982) 'Expertise in problem-solving'. In R. J. Sternberg, (ed.) *Advances in the Psychology of Human Intelligence* vol. 1. Hillsdale, N.J.: Erlbaum.

Rumbelhart, G. (1980) 'Schemata. The Building Blocks of Cognition.' *Theoretical Issues in Reading and Comprehension*, Hillsdale, NJ:

Selye, H. (1952) *The Story of the Adaptation Syndrome*. Montreal: Acta.

Schank, R. (1975) 'Using knowledge to understand'. *Theoretical Issues in Natural Language*, New Jersey:

Schank, R. and Abelson, R. (1977) *Scripts, Plans, Goals and Understanding*. Laurence Erlbaum Associates.

Schrieber, G., Breuker, J. A., Bredeweg, B. and Wielinga, B. J. (1988) 'Modelling in KBS development' In *Proceedings of the European Knowledge Acquisition Workshop (EKAW '88)* J. H. Boose, B. R. Caines, and M. Linster, (eds). Sankt Augusta, West Germany GMD, pp. 7. 1–7.15.

Shaw, M. 'Acquisition of personal knowledge'. *International Journal of Policy Analysis and Information Systems*. vol. 4. 4.

Sloman, A. (1978) 'What is conceptual analysis?' *The Computer Revolution in Philosophy* ch. 4, pp. 84–102.

Smith, E. and Miller, F. (1978) 'Limits of perception of cognitive processes. A reply to Nisbett and Wilson'. *Psychology Review*, vol. 85 (4), pp. 355–62.

Smith, N. W. (1968) 'On the origin of conflict types'. *Psychological Research*. vol. 18, pp. 229–32.

Sowa, J. F. (1984) *Conceptual Structures: Information processing in mind and machine*. Reading, MA: Addison-Wesley.

Sowa, J. F. (1981) 'A conceptual schema for knowledge based systems'. Proc. Workshop on Data Abstraction, Databases, and Conceptual Modelling, SIGMOD Record vol. 11 (2), pp. 193–5.

Sowa, J. F. (1968) Intentions, Extensions, and Symbols. Conceptual Structures. A Model for Language, unpublished manuscript.

Stevens, A., Collins, A., and Goldin, S. (1979). 'Misconceptions in students understandings'. *Journal of Man-Machine Studies*, vol. 11, pp. 145–56.

Sturzda, Paltin (1983) 'From Data Base to Knowledge Base: Artificial Intelligence with an IBM Data Dictionary'. Proc. International Conference on Computer Capacity Management, New Orleans.

Tulvrig, E. (1985) 'How many memory systems are there?' *American Psychologist*, vol. 40 (4), pp. 385–98.

Tversky, A. and Kahneman, D. (1974) 'Judgement under uncertainty: Heuristics and biases'. *Science*, vol. 185, pp. 1124–31.

Veryard, R. (1986) 'What are methodologies good for?' *Data Processing*, vol. 17, no. 6, July/August.

Watzlawick, P. J. (1964) *Anthology of Human Communication*. Palo Alto, Cal.: Science and Behaviour Books.

Wellbank, M. (1983) 'A review of knowledge acquisition techniques for expert systems'. British Telecommunications Research Laboratories Technical Report. Martlesham Heath, Ipswich, England.

Wielinga, B. J. and Breuker, J. A. Methods of Acquisition and Analysis Technique for Knowledge Based Systems: (1983) *Report 1.1 Memorandum 10*. Esprit Project 12; (1983) *Report 1.2 Memorandum 12*. Esprit Project 12; (1983) *Report 1.3a Memorandum 23*. Esprit Project 12; (1984) *Report 1.5 Memorandum 28*. Esprit Project 12; (1987) *The Statcons Case Study. Deliverable E2.3. Task F2. Esprit Project 1098; (1987) Towards a Design Methodology for KBS Deliverable D8*. Esprit Project 1098; (1988) *Knowledge Acquisition for Expert*

Systems. Esprit Project 1098; (1988) *Modality. KADS.* Esprit Project 1098; (1989) *Models of Expertise in Knowledge Acquisition.* Esprit Project 1098; (1989) *Design and Implementation of a Configuration Task.* Esprit Project 1098; (1989) *A KADS Design Description Language. Deliverable B7.* Esprit Project 1098; (1989) *A KADS Approach to KBS Design.* Esprit Project, 1098; (1989) *Synthesis Report, KADS.* Esprit Project, 1098.

Wielinga, B. J. and Schrieber, G. (1989) In *Research and Development in Expert Systems '89.* 9th Annual Conference of the British Computer Society Specialists Group on Expert Systems. 20–2 September. (ed. Nigel Shadbolt). London.

Wielinga, B. J., Akkermans, H., Schrieber, G. and Balsder, J. (1989). Knowledge Acquisition Perspective on Knowledge-Level Models. Paper for the Banff Knowledge Acquisition Workshop. KAW.

Wielinga, B. J. and Breuker, J. A. (1985) 'Interpretation of verbal data for knowledge acquisition'. In *Advances in Artificial Intelligence* (ed T. O'Shea). Amsterdam: North Holland, pp. 3–12.

Wielinga, B. J. and Breuker, J. A. (1986) 'Models of Expertise'. *Proceedings of Seventh European Conference on Artificial Intelligence. (ECAI '86),* Brighton, July vol. 1, pp. 306–18.

Weinberg, G. 'Motivation, training and experience'. *The Psychology of Computer Programming.* New York: Van Nostrand Reingold Co.

Wilkins, D. C., Buchanan, B. G. and Clancey, W. J. (1904) 'Inferring an expert's reasoning by watching'. Heuristic Planning Project Report No. HPP-84-29. Department of Computer Science, Stanford University, Stanford CA, USA.

Wittgenstein, Ludwig. (1953) *Philosophical Investigations.* Oxford: Basil Blackwell.

Wilson, M. D. 'Task analysis for knowledge acquisition'. In *Knowledge Acquisition for Engineering Applications,* C. J. Paveliu and M. P. Wilson, (eds) pp. 68–83.

Woods, A. W. (1983) 'What's important about knowledge representation?' Institute of Electric and Electronic Engineers, *Computer.* vol. 16, pp. 22–9.

Woolnough, Mike (1988) An expert, for his permission to use for this book an excerpt from a transcript. The Prudential Corporation, High Holborn, London.

Wright, G. and Ayton, P. (1987) 'Eliciting and modelling expert knowledge'. *Decision Support Systems,* vol. 3, (1), pp. 13–26.

Young, G. (1982) *Automatic Schema Acquisition in a Natural Language Environment.* American Association of Artificial Intelligence.

Young, R. M. and Gammack, J. G. (1987) 'Role of psychological techniques and intermediate representations in knowledge elicitation.' *Proceedings of the First European Workshop on Knowledge Acquisition for Knowledge-Based Systems.* Reading, UK, 2–3 September, Reading University, Reading, Section D7.

Further reading

Abelson, R. (1967) 'Psychological Implication' In *Theories of Cognitive Consistency: A sourcebook*, (eds) R. Abelson *et al*. Chicago: Rand McNally.

Anjewierden, A. (1987) 'Knowledge acquisition tools' *AI Communications* vol. 0 (1), pp. 29–38 (August 1987). Also in *Proceedings of the First European Workshop on Knowledge Acquisition for Knowledge-based Systems*, Reading, UK. 2–3 September, 1987. Reading, Reading University, section E2, pp. 1–12.

Arkes, H. R. and Freedman, M. R. (1984) 'A demonstration of the cost and benefits of memory'. *Memory and Cognition*, vol. 12, pp. 84–9.

Argyle, M. (1967) *The Psychology of Interpersonal Behaviour*. Harmondsworth, Middlesex: Penguin Books.

Baddeley, A. (1976) *The Psychology of Memory*. New York: Basic Books.

Bainbridge, L. (1979) 'Verbal reports as evidence of the process operator's knowledge'. *International Journal Of Man Machine Studies*. vol. 11, pp. 411–36.

Bartol, R. and Ku, N. (1980) 'Thinking aloud during reading'. *Scandinavian Journal of Psychology*, vol. 21, pp. 123–32.

Boose, J. H. (1985) 'A knowledge acquisition program for expert systems based on personal construct psychology'. *International Journal of Man Machine Studies*, vol. 23, pp. 495–525.

Boulay, B., O'Shea, T. and Monk, J. (1981) 'The black box inside the glass box'. Presenting computer concepts to novices. *International Journal of Man-Machine Studies*, vol. 14, pp. 237–49.

Bower, G., Black, J. and Turner, T. (1979) 'Scripts in memory for text'. *Cognitive Psychology*, vol. 11, pp. 117–220.

Cattell, R., and Kline, P. (1977) *Scientific Analysis of Personality and Motivation*. New York: Academic Press.

Chi, M. T. H., Glaser, R. and Farr, M. (1988) 'The nature of expertise'. Hillsdale, NJ: Erlbaum.

Chandrasekaran, B. (1986) 'Generic tasks in knowledge based reasoning: high level building blocks for expert system design'. *Institute of Electrical and Electronic Engineers Expert*, vol. 1 (3), pp. 23–30.

Coleman, T. C. (1989) *Expert Systems for the D.P. Manager*. Manchester: National Computer Center Publications.

Cowen, E. (1952) 'The influence of varying degrees of psychological stress on problem solving rigidity'. *Journal of Abnormal and Social Psychology*, vol. 47, pp. 512–19.

Craik, Kenneth, J. W. (1943) *The Nature of Explanation*. Cambridge: Cambridge University Press.

De Marco (1978) *Structured Analysis and System Specification*. New York: Yourdon Press.

Dermer, J. (1973) 'Cognitive characteristics and the perceived importance of information'. *The Accounting Review*, July, pp. 511–19.

Di Sessa, A. (1983) 'Phenomenology and the evolution of intuition'. In *Mental Models* (eds.) D. Gentner and A. Stevens. London: Laurence Erlbaum Associates. Ch. 2, pp. 15–33.

Easton, Geoff. (1982) *Learning from Case Histories*. Hemel Hempstead: Prentice Hall International.

Einhorn, H. (1974) 'Learning form experience and sub-optimal rules in decision-making'. In *Judgement under Uncertainty: Heuristics and Biases*, (eds) D. Kahneman, P. Slovic and A. Tversky. Cambridge: Cambridge University Press.

Ericsson, K. and Simon, H. (1980) 'Verbal reports as data'. *Psychological Review*, vol. 87, no. 3, pp. 215–51.

Feigenbaum, E. A. (1977) 'The art of artificial intelligence'. Themes and case studies of knowledge engineering. In *Proc. IJCAI-77*, (5), 1014–29.

Fiest, J. (1985) *Theories of Personality*. London: Holt Saunders.

Fishoff, Baruch (1982) 'For those condemned to study the past: Heuristics and Biases in Hindsight' In *Judgement under Uncertainty: Heuristics and Biases* (eds.) A. Tversky, P. Slovic, D. Kahneman. Cambridge: Cambridge University Press, Part VI, 23, pp. 335–54.

Fox, J. (1980) 'Making decisions under the influence of memory' *Psychological Review*, vol. 87, no. 2, 190–211.

Frenkel-Brunswik, E. (1948) 'Tolerance towards ambiguity as a personality variable.' *American Psychologist*, vol. 3, p. 868.

Friend, K. (1982) 'Stress and performance of subjective work-load v time urgency'. *Personal Psychology*, vol. 35, no. 3, pp. 623–33.

Gammack, J. and Young, R. (1985) *Psychological Techniques for Eliciting Expert Knowledge*, ed. M. A. Bramer. Cambridge: Cambridge University Press, pp. 105–12.

Gevarter, W. B. (1987) 'The nature and evaluation of commerce in expert system building tools'. *Computer*, vol. 20, (5), 24–41.

Goldstein, K. M. and Blackman, S. (1978) *Cognitive Style: five approaches and relevant research*. New York: John Wiley & Sons.

Green, R. and Wood, S. (1984) 'Expert knowledge elicitation or how to grow trees'. *Expert Systems*, pp. 272–6.

Hart, A. (1985) 'The role of induction in knowledge elicitation' *Expert Systems*, vol. 2 (1), pp. 24–8.

Haviland, S. and Clark, H. (1974) 'What's new? Acquiring information as a process in comprehension'. *Journal of Verbal Learning and Verbal Behaviour*, vol. 13, pp. 514–21.

Hawkins, D. (1983) 'An analysis of expert thinking'. *International Journal of Man-Machine Studies*, vol. 18 (1), pp. 1–47.

Hayes-Roth, B. and Wason, C. (1979) 'Configural effects in human memory. The superiority of memory over information sources for inference verification'. *Cognitive Science*, vol. 3, pp. 119–40.

Hayes-Roth, F. Klahr, P. and Mostow, D. (1985) 'Advice-taking and knowledge refining. An iterative view of skill acquisition'. In J. Anderson *Cognitive Skill and their Acquisition*, Hillsdale, N.J: Laurence Erlbaum Associates.

Heider, F. (1946) 'Attitudes and cognitive organisation'. *Journal of psychology*, vol. 21, pp. 107-12.

Jackendoff, Ray (1987) 'On Beyond Zebra: The relation of linguistic and visual information'. *Cognition* vols. 25-7. Brandeis University, Elsevier Science Publishers, B. V., The Netherlands.

Johnson-Laird, P. and Wason, P. (1969) 'A theoretical analysis of insight into a reasoning task'. In *Thinking* (eds) Johnson-Laird, P. and Wason, P., Cambridge: Cambridge University Press.

Joshi, A., Webber, B. and Sag, I. (eds) (1981) *Elements of Discourse Understanding*. Cambridge: Cambridge University Press.

Kaplan, S. J. (1978) 'Indirect responses to loaded questions'. Proceedings of TINLAP — 2 ACM, pp. 202-9.

Kitto, C. M. and Boose, J. H. (1987) 'Heuristics for expert transfer: an implementation of a dialogue manager for knowledge acquisition'. *International Journal of Man-Machine Studies*, vol. 26 (2), pp. 183-202.

Kolodner, J. (1983) 'Maintaining organisation in dynamic long term memory'. *Cognitive Science*, vol. 7, pp. 243-80.

Korman, B. (1978) *Hads: The power of awareness*. New York: Sunridge Press.

Larkin, J. H., McDermott, J., Simon, D. P. and Simon, H. A. (1980) 'Expert and novice performance in solving physics problems'. *Science*, vol. 20, p. 208.

Mehrabian, A. (1971) *Silent Messages*. Behot, California: Wadsworth.

Neale, I. M. (1988) 'First generation expert systems: a review of knowledge acquisition methodologies'. *The Knowledge Engineering Review*, vol. 2, pp. 105-45. (ARIES at City, Room CM355, The City University, London, EC1V0HB).

Newell, A. and Simon, H. A. (1972) 'Human Problem Solving'. Englewood Cliffs, NJ: Prentice Hall.

Reboh, Rene (1983) 'Extracting useful advice from conflicting expertise'. SRI International, or In: *Proceedings of the Eighth International Joint Conference on Artificial Intelligence*, pp. 145-50.

Riesbeck, C. (1975) *Conceptual Information Processing*, (ed.) R. Shank. Amsterdam: North-Holland Publishing Company.

Rokeach, M. (1960) *The Open and Closed Mind*. New York: Basic Books.

Schwab, A., Jordan, G. *et al.* (1986) 'Protecting Technology through Litigation'. *The Computer Lawyer*, vol. 3, no. 4, April.

Searle, J. (1983) *Intentionality*. Cambridge: Cambridge University Press.

Segall, M., Cambell, D. and Herskovitis, M. (1966) *The Influence of Culture on Visual Perception*. Indianopolis: Bobbs-Merill.

Shaw, M. L. G. and Gaines, B. R. (1987) 'Kitten. Knowledge initiation and transfer tools for experts and novices'. *International Journal of Man Machine Studies*, vol. 27, pp. 251-80.

Slovic, P. (1972) 'From Shakespeare to Simon: Speculations and some evidence about man's ability to process information'. *Oregon Research Institute Research Bulletin*, vol. 12, p. 2.

Sternberg, S. (1979) 'Memory Scanning, Mental processes revealed by reaction time experiments'. *American Scientist*, 57, vol. 4, pp. 421-57.

Thouless, R. H. *Straight and Crooked Thinking*. London: Pan Books.

White, G. M. (1975) 'Conceptual analysis'. In *the Owl of Minerva*, (eds C. J. Bontempo and S. J. Odel), New York: McGraw-Hill, pp. 103–17.

Wilensky, R. (1983) *Planning and Understanding*. Reading, MA: Addison-Wesley.

Winston, P. G. (1986) 'Models rule. Winston warns'. *Reports in Expert Systems User*, vol. 2 (9), p. 5.

Young, R. and Gammack, J. (1987) 'Role of psychological techniques and intermediate representations in knowledge elicitation' In *Proceedings of the first European Workshop on Knowledge Acquisition for Knowledge Based Systems*, Reading: Reading University, Section D7.

Zakay, Dan (1982) 'Reliability of information as a potential threat to the accessibility of information'. *Transactions on Systems, Man and Cybernetics*, vol. SMC12, no. 4. Institute of Electric and Electronic Engineers.

Index